Eighteenth-Century
Venetian Drawings
from the Corer Museum

85. FRANCESCO GUARDI: A Porch with Figures

Eighteenth-Century Venetian Drawings

from the Correr Museum

CIRCULATED BY THE SMITHSONIAN INSTITUTION
1963-1964

National Gallery of Art   WASHINGTON, D.C.

The Museum of Fine Arts   HOUSTON, TEXAS

Los Angeles County Museum of Art   LOS ANGELES, CALIFORNIA

California Palace of the Legion of Honor   SAN FRANCISCO, CALIFORNIA

SMITHSONIAN PUBLICATION NO. 4521

PRODUCED BY
THE MERIDEN GRAVURE COMPANY
AND
THE STINEHOUR PRESS

Acknowledgments

THIS EXHIBITION of eighteenth-century Venetian Drawings from the Correr Museum in Venice is the ninth in a series of old master drawings exhibitions circulated since 1952 by the Smithsonian Institution Traveling Exhibition Service, and the third from Italy. Carefully selected by one of the outstanding scholars in the field of Venetian art, Professor Terisio Pignatti, the exhibition consists of 120 works by forty-two artists including such great masters as Canaletto, Guardi, Tiepolo, and Piazzetta, and others by lesser-known but nonetheless extremely fine artists who deserve to be studied more closely.

We are deeply grateful to the Italian Government and the Fine Arts Commissions of Rome and Venice for permitting the precious drawings to travel to this country, and we would like to thank the many officials and museum directors whose co-operation and understanding helped make this show a reality: first of all, the Mayor of Venice, Ing. Giovanni Favaretto Fisca, and his Arts Councillor, Professor Mario De Biasi; Professor Bruno Molajoli and Dr. Guglielmo Triches in Rome; Professor Pietro Zampetti, Professor Giovanni Mariacher, Dr. Giovanni Paccagnini, Dr. Francesco Valcanover, Professor Giuseppe Mazzariol, and Mr. Michael Levey, all of whom contributed generously of their time and advice to the organization of the exhibition which is the first of its kind to be shown here.

We are indebted to Professor Antonio Morassi and Mr. Italico Brass for allowing us to include four of their drawings which are at present on loan to the Correr Museum.

Our special thanks go to Professor Terisio Pignatti, Vice Director of the Correr Museum and Keeper of Prints and Drawings, for the difficult task of making a representative selection from the thousands of drawings in his care and for writing the exhibition catalogue —the first publication in this century on the Museum's drawing collection.

The Board of Directors of the Cini Foundation of Venice, through Professor Vittore Branca, Secretary General, and Dr. Alessandro Bettagno, Secretary, has given us invaluable assistance by contributing a new set of photographs made expressly for the catalogue by Umberto Rossi in Venice.

His Excellency Sergio Fenoaltea, Ambassador of Italy, has graciously consented to sponsor the exhibition throughout its tour and to open it officially at the National Gallery of Art.

We would like to acknowledge the assistance of the Meriden Gravure Company which designed and printed the catalogue.

Recognition should also be given to the Smithsonian staff, and especially to Penelope Billings, Nancy Curtis, and Mary Cole Dickerman, for their constant and devoted efforts in attending to the numerous details of organizing and circulating this show.

ANNEMARIE H. POPE
Smithsonian Institution

Introduction

Tiepolo, Guardi, Longhi, Piazzetta, Canaletto: these are only a few among many artists whose works are included in this impressive exhibition, the first on the subject of Venetian eighteenth-century drawings. Yet, from the popular viewpoint, these names represent a summary, but still penetrating portrait of a culture, an artistic world, and a city. This city is Venice in the settecento, her last century as an independent state and perhaps her most glorious one in humanities and poetry. This portrait, conveyed to us in thousands of ways, is more clearly delineated than any from the other centuries of Venice's existence.

Perhaps its image has been preserved because so much of the city's past still remains close to us: gondolas and canals, crowded *fondamente* with lazy boys in the sun, and the Piazza San Marco (the only square in Venice, all the others being *campi*) with processions of foreigners, and the boats bobbing on the water along the Riva degli Schiavoni.

But perhaps these familiar sights evoke memories of the past because they correspond to an inner image created by many artists' portraits of the Venetian eighteenth century, a time beloved and dreamed about like a youthful fancy. This glorious century was captured by Canaletto and Guardi, Tiepolo, Longhi, and Rosalba and still lives in their works, which themselves added to the superb décor of the period. Modern connoisseurship and taste, a romantic echo of the past, and the reminiscences of everyday sights have indeed made the Venetian eighteenth century one of the most inviting centuries in art.

To re-establish in this exhibition some of the high points of this period is, we think, an exciting event.

Is there anyone who does not know that Venice in the eighteenth century recovered her lost Golden Age, profiting by an extraordinary stock of great artists and by an especially favorable social milieu? Is it also realized that the excellence of Venetian art in this period is not limited to painting alone but extends as well to prints and drawings?

The early years of the eighteenth century witnessed a revival of all the arts in Venice, after a period of decline during the seicento. Traveling painters took the voice of Venice everywhere in Italy and Europe. Sebastiano and Marco Ricci, Pellegrini, Amigoni, and

Diziani were working in the first decades of the century in Rome and Naples, in England, the Low Countries, France, Germany, and Poland. Their drawings assume an international flavor instead of continuing the late seventeenth-century themes of the previous generation of Venetians—Zanchi, Carneo, Celesti, Lazzarini, Molinari, or Balestra.

Sebastiano Ricci (1659–1734) was the first artist in Venice to begin the transition from late Baroque style to Rococo. Some of his drawings towards the end of the seventeenth century indicate that he began in the traditions of the Carracci and also recall his contact with Luca Giordano and Solimena. This valuable academic education left its imprint on Ricci's drawings into the eighteenth century, when he was able to abandon his plastic style for a vigorous and decorative *rocaille*. Considering his famous albums at Windsor Castle and the Gallerie dell'Accademia in Venice, it can be said without a doubt that he ranks among the best draftsmen of his time.

Ricci was deeply indebted as a draftsman to *Gian Antonio Pellegrini* (1675–1741). Pellegrini liberated himself from the plastic seicento tradition and attained a painterly style of open forms, from which light and space seemed to emanate. His evolution represents the essence of the change from Baroque to Rococo. In his early drawings, Pellegrini shows an affinity to Pagani through fluent lines that precisely define the outlines of his forms. An important achievement of modern criticism was the discovery of a group of Pellegrini's early drawings in the Düsseldorf Museum, where they had lain unnoticed under an incorrect attribution to Molinari (Bettagno, 1959). Later, in 1700, after having been in the circle of Baciccio in Rome, he passed through a period of whirling lines to reach the open forms of his maturity —when his pen strokes, applied in contrast to light paper, create scintillating effects, and the mood is fresh and swirling like a cool waterfall in an Arcadian garden.

This basic permutation in Pellegrini's style evolves even further, during his sojourn in Britain (1708–13), when he came in contact with the work of Rembrandt and van Dyck. While in Britain, he expanded his graphic expression by a new and characteristic use of dark spots of wash in vivid contrast to light areas sparked by erratic lines. Afterwards, when he visited the Low Countries and Germany, he had further occasion to see Flemish and Dutch painting (Pignatti, 1959). What are his drawings in the Mauritshuis in The Hague, if not actually Venetian interpretations of Rembrandt? (Similarly, an acquaintance with the work of the Dutch master was fundamental to Tiepolo's development.) In Pellegrini's last drawings, his lines dissolve into dazzling atmosphere, and all interest in modeling is lost.

The formative years of *Gian Antonio Guardi* (1699–1761) coincide with Pellegrini's late period, and the draftsmanship of Guardi in his early figure drawings of the thirties could even be confused with Pellegrini's. Recently, it has been established that Guardi often copied from Pellegrini paintings (Morassi, 1958). From his early career, under the strong influence of Pellegrini, Gian Antonio reached the height of Rococo expression. His early relationship with the older master takes on additional importance because it seems to be the only way to make the difficult distinction between Gian Antonio's figure paintings and the few figure sketches by his brother Francesco, who was mainly a *vedute* painter (Pignatti, 1957).

Modern research has been able to establish only a few certain facts about the secondary draftsmen of the early eighteenth century. For instance, drawings have been attributed to *Nicola Grassi* (1682–1748) solely on the evidence of old inscriptions, without stylistic confirmation. For the first time, one can say that a sheet included in this exhibition seems to belong unquestionably to this artist's oeuvre; it shows an interesting relationship to the first wave of Rococo draftsmanship, which I have just described. However, Grassi's similarity to Ricci and Pellegrini is marked by a sort of provincial stiffness, which places him with a group of painters working in Venice but also connected with the northeast provinces. Among these, Bencovich and Pittoni are the most important.

Federico Bencovich (1677–1756) is at present not well-known as a draftsman. In the few drawings attributed to him with certainty (two of which are in the Correr), he is linked to the late seventeenth-century tradition, in the manner of Zanchi or Celesti. Sometimes he seems to strive for the chiaroscuro effects that he employs in his paintings. In examples of his later work, he adopted the hatching typical of Ricci's modeling.

We have sufficient knowledge of the various drawings by *Gian Battista Pittoni* (1687–1767), from the first sketch to the finished drawings or collector's album pieces (Pallucchini, 1945). Stylistically, Pittoni's drawings proclaim his academic training, probably within the traditions of the Carracci. His delicate touch also has something in common with Maratta, whom he might have known through Balestra, his teacher. In his finished drawings, usually executed in black and white chalk on brown paper, we can detect the style of Ricci, who also influenced his paintings, and of Piazzetta in the nuances of his modeling. Pittoni's prolific output of drawings—although responsible for his considerable renown—was not advantageous to the quality of his work, which frequently was sacrificed to more practical demands. Though we often regret some lack of taste in his drawings, he obtains through the subtlety of his oil sketches one of the most distinguished positions in the Venetian settecento.

How extraordinary that only a few drawings have been handed down to us from such painters of international reputation as *Jacopo Amigoni* (1682–1752) and Crosato! Except for the large series of portraits on blue paper, ascribed to Amigoni's English period (1729–39), we are almost ignorant of his compositional drawings; the one belonging to the Correr—here exhibited for the first time—can only be considered a starting point for further consideration. Knowing that Amigoni was born in Naples, we might expect to detect in his graphic style the influence of Giordano's fluid lines. Further research on the characteristics of

9

his drawings could be based on observations concerning his painting technique. In his great decorative enterprises in England, Germany, and Spain, he enriched his chromatic values, following the example of Balestra and Ricci; simultaneously, when he began using bright colors, he displayed a tendency to model with almost Neoclassic coolness. In his small Arcadian canvases, however, he retained the vibrant spirit of the Venetian Rococo; their color is more loosely applied and subtler.

The artistic evolution of *Gian Battista Crosato* (c. 1685–1758) is similar. That he too received a classical training in the region between Rome and Emilia can be assumed if we judge by the brilliant and imposing color of his frescoes in Piedmont and the Veneto. To date, only a few drawings have been attributed to Crosato; the only one in the Correr seems related to the large frescoes and also suggests a contact with Ricci and his school, largely active in Venice.

Without hesitation we consider *Gaspare Diziani* (1689–1767) to be among the best draftsmen of Venice. The largest, and relatively unknown, collection of his drawings is housed at the Correr. Diziani is considered a follower of Ricci in his paintings but has a distinct style in his drawings, which have a crispness in their *rocaille* lines, unfolding and contracting in tireless involutions, as opposed to the characteristic shimmering and silver, or gold-green, iridescent color of his paintings. The proximity of his graphic technique to the open forms of Pellegrini and G. A. Guardi sometimes leads to confusion.

The development of Diziani's draftsmanship can be followed through many certain drawings connected with dated paintings. However, a problem sometimes arises because of his tendency to revert to earlier stylistic devices, in both his pencil and red chalk sketches, as well as in his more finished pen and wash drawings and large album sheets for collectors. His drawings are now at the Albertina, Budapest, and Hermitage museums, but the major group belongs to the Correr.

Only in its formative stages does Diziani's style resemble that of Ricci, with characteristic hatching that has often been confused with Fontebasso's etching manner. In his late drawings in the sixties, Diziani is unquestionably a *rocaille* draftsman, ranking with the best— Pellegrini, G. A. Guardi, and even Tiepolo. Recent criticism has separated from the father's work several sheets by his son Giuseppe Diziani (1732–1803), distinguished by their shell-like, dotted lines (Muraro, 1957).

Because of the richness of his interests, Diziani's drawings dominate the middle decades of the eighteenth century and had considerable influence on his contemporaries. His inventiveness and delightful imagination are typically graphic, so that we are tempted to admire his drawings more than his paintings of the same subjects.

Eclecticism—standing midway between Pellegrini and Ricci on the one hand and

Diziani on the other—is perhaps the characteristic feature of the middle generation, exemplified by a few certain drawings by *Mattia Bortoloni* (1695–1750); *Anton Maria Zanetti* (1679–1767), noted for his Parmigianino-like chiaroscuri and caricatures in Windsor Library; *Gerolamo Brusaferro* (1680–1760); and *Gian Battista Marcuola* (1711–80). Recent literature—especially the latest exhibition catalogues published by the Fondazione Giorgio Cini in Venice, has defined a few characteristics of these artists. While these painters are usually considered to be in the academic tradition of the late Baroque period, their drawings are in fact far more advanced than their paintings. What convincing evidence of the basic importance of draftsmanship as the secret to the artist's vocabulary!

Francesco Fontebasso (1709–69) deserves at least a paragraph in the history of Venetian eighteenth-century draftsmanship for his achievements both as draftsman and as printmaker. In his etchings, the majority of which were executed in his youth, Fontebasso employs sharp lines that define outlines of solids and, characteristically, creates chiaroscuro effects with cross hatching. His fluent and uninterrupted line reveals his academic education in the Bolognese and Ricci manner. In many of his finished drawings, such as the Correr, Hermitage, and Albertina album pieces, he shows a distinct personality, closer to Ricci—and subsequently to Tiepolo—than to the open manner of Pellegrini (to whom we have been able to relate Diziani in his most advanced work).

Until recently, we lacked sufficient graphic documents for three important painters, whose main output was in fresco: *Bartolomeo Tarsia* (1711–65), *Jacopo Marieschi* (1711–94), and *Jacopo Guarana* (1720–1808). However, drawings in the Correr now given to them indicate that they were followers of Ricci. Guarana seems to have been a very good draftsman, with a free and charming style that is comparable to the delicate chiaroscuro or grisaille details in his large fresco decorations.

The oeuvre of Piazzetta has often been studied and is generally well known. The main problem of recent literature has been to distinguish between the work of the master and the production of his large workshop, which incorporated *Egidio dall'Oglio* (1705–84), *Domenico Maggiotto* (1713–93), *Francesco Cappella* (1714–84), and *Giuseppe Angeli* (1710–98) (Pallucchini, 1934, 1956).

The graphic output of *Gian Battista Piazzetta* (1683–1754) is multiform. It ranges from academic nudes for the *scuola di pittura*, which were later reproduced by Pitteri in the famous printbook of 1760, down to collector's pieces, generally half-length saints or heads of handsome peasants in the Arcadian convention, which are housed for the most part at Windsor and the Accademia in Venice.

The typical Piazzetta medium is black chalk heightened with white on gray-brown or blue paper, a technique that emphasizes modeling and luminosity. Piazzetta worked exten-

11

sively on book illustrations, subsequently etched by Pitteri and Cattini, to mention only two of the best artists who made prints after his work. Large collections of his preliminary drawings in red pencil are in the Hermitage, the Biblioteca Reale in Turin, and the Morgan Library in New York. As yet, there is no adequate explanation for the counterproofs, reverse copies obtained by pressing paper down on the moistened originals, which were often made by the master himself during his working process. A new and still growing body of research on Piazzetta is being devoted to his compositional studies in pen or pencil, which for a long time have been totally unknown. Now we know that Piazzetta used tight and structural lines, sketching forms with flashing touches (Pignatti, 1957; Pallucchini, 1959–60).

A singular position in Venetian eighteenth-century draftsmanship is held by *Pietro Longhi* (1702–85), most of whose drawings are in the Correr. They are all similar in technique and media (pencil and black chalk heightened with white on grayish or brown paper) and for the most part were used as preparatory studies for the small canvases. In these studies, Longhi was apparently concerned with recording historical setting and costume more than personalities. The unique aspect of these drawings is that they are always based on reality, as shown by the notations on colors and light.

The contrast between Pietro Longhi's draftsmanship and all contemporary Venetian examples is startling. Should we dare to propose that a closer link might be found with contemporary French drawings—by Watteau, Pater, Lancret, or even some sheets by Chardin? It seems relevant that such an observation has been previously made by connoisseurs with unquestionable taste, such as Mariette or the Goncourts. For some time it has been recognized that Pietro Longhi was among the first Venetians to adopt attitudes of the Enlightenment, which originated in France. By comparing contemporary writings by Baretti or Goldoni, who was Longhi's friend, we can easily see that they were motivated by the same critical attitude toward eighteenth-century society as was Longhi. But an adequate explanation of why his graphic style sometimes has more in common with the French than the Venetian manner still needs to be made. Perhaps the link is provided by Flipart, a native Parisian who joined Longhi's atelier after 1737, imitated his style, and made etchings after his paintings.

The latest studies on Longhi have separated from the father's work some drawings by his son *Alessandro Longhi* (1733–1813). Although a pupil of the pastel painter *Giuseppe Nogari* (1699–1763), Alessandro's manner is so closely related to Pietro's in some drawings that it becomes confusing. However, he was not a born draftsman; this is confirmed by his paintings, which rely for their value on delicate distinctions of color, and by his prints, marked more by the sensitivity of one accustomed to a brush than by the crisp quality of a true etcher.

Some artists working throughout the eighteenth century may be grouped together by their common use of landscape subject matter. First among them was *Marco Ricci* (1676–

12

1730), Sebastiano's nephew, an outstanding etcher and draftsman. Often, his landscape sketches are in effect paintings, as is the case with his gouaches or tempera paintings on parchment, the largest portion of which are now conserved at Windsor. He also worked frequently in pen, sketching ideas for figure compositions, stage designs—especially during his first English visit, 1708–10—and landscapes; the latter type were preparations for etchings or pieces to be sold to collectors. Many of these drawings were bound in albums; in the nineteenth century, two—very likely volumes in the possession of Consul Joseph Smith—were broken up into many hundreds of sheets and sold. The largest collection of Marco Ricci drawings is housed at Windsor Castle, which has nearly one hundred and fifty works in addition to the caricatures from the Smith album. Considering the latter examples, it would also appear that Marco Ricci was one of the first artists to take up caricature, a genre favored by Ghezzi in Rome and Tiepolo in Venice.

Much discussion has recently taken place concerning Ricci's education, and many important studies have been devoted to his graphic style (Blunt, 1957). A sort of classic atmosphere emanates from a true drawing by Marco; the crisp hatching and the transparency of his washes, in typical golden-brown inks, suggest the early Titian or Domenico Campagnola. No doubt Ricci was inspired by Salvator Rosa, whose classical works he saw as a youth on journeys to Rome and Naples (Pallucchini, 1961). Possibly he was also acquainted with Poussin, whose warm and mellow quality he sometimes duplicates in his drawings. The most important thing is that Marco Ricci, by uniting the best of Renaissance and seventeenth-century naturalism, revived in Venice the bright vision of nature and space that had been obscured by artistic decay during the seventeenth century. Thus, Marco Ricci paves the way for the etchings and drawings of Canaletto.

The introduction of the typical, southern *pittura di rovine*, or pictures of ruins, antiquities, and classical architecture, into the Venetian region is one of the consequences of Rosa's influence on Marco Ricci. A second is the renewal of interest in *macchiette*, or stylized figure sketches, which particularly inspired the battle painters that followed Callot and the Borgognones.

It is not arbitrary to connect with Ricci's draftsmanship a few examples by the perspective painter *Antonio Visentini* (1688–1782), better known as a book-illustrator and an etcher who copied Canaletto than as an original artist. The majority of his drawings are at Windsor.

Among the *battaglisti*, painters of battle scenes, *Francesco Simonini* (1686–1753) was influenced in his drawings by Ricci. Simonini comes from a specialized branch of this genre painting, having been a direct follower of the famous Monti. Many drawings confirm the tradition that *Giuseppe Zais* (1709–84), another battle painter, was Simonini's pupil. Zais's

13

best works, however, were landscapes under the influence of Ricci, crisp and humorous drawings done in pen, wash, or tempera.

Francesco Zuccarelli (1702–88) is slightly older than Zais. His early training in Rome left a trace of Cortona and even of Maratta's mellowness in his loose strokes and painterly shading. Subsequent experience in England and France led him to the highest refinements in his graphic technique, sometimes achieving the effects of pastel and eventually obtaining a coolness that foreshadowed Neoclassicism. A large number of his drawings is known in various media—in red or black pencil, chalk, or wash, frequently colored or accented with tempera. They are in Windsor Castle, the British Museum, the Uffizi, and the Morassi collection in Milan.

A significant portion of eighteenth-century Venetian drawings in public and private collections is the work of *vedute* painters. These drawings, depicting scenes of Venice with meticulous care, have always been in great demand; consequently they were produced in large quantity and were frequently copied. Also, they were more carefully preserved than other types of drawings, even by people who could not appreciate anything but their subject, because they evoked the magic of the city of lagoons.

The *vedute* genre, not totally new in Venice, flourished there in the eighteenth century. *Johan Richter* (1665–1745), a Swedish painter and long-time resident of Venice, was an early *vedute* painter along with *Luca Carlevaris* (1663–1730). The few sure drawings by Richter are somewhat similar to Ricci. Carlevaris can be considered nothing more than a mediocre etcher and an often clumsy draftsman, with the possible exception of his work in some drawings belonging to the Correr, the Victoria and Albert Museum, and the British Museum. Obviously, he is handicapped by comparison with Canaletto, Bellotto, and Francesco Guardi.

Antonio Canal, called *Canaletto*, (1697–1768) is one of the universal geniuses in the graphic arts who created masterpieces in both prints and drawings. His drawings were of two categories: functional studies for the preparation of *vedute* paintings, and finished drawings made for sale to collectors. Of the first type, we have many documentary drawings sketched on the spot, such as the sketchbook at the Accademia or the Viggiano series (part of which is also at the Accademia), and other pieces like the one at the Fogg Museum. I feel, with good evidence, that Canaletto used these sketches (and probably even more summary ones done on the spot, possibly with the aid of a portable camera obscura) to make up his Venetian views, whether they were to become album drawings in pen or gouache, or prints, or paintings. The role of the optical device in this work is still open to question (Pignatti, 1958; Ragghianti, 1959; Gioseffi, 1959).

The most important group of Canaletto drawings is of the second, "collector" type. Apart from those at the British Museum, the finest group is at Windsor Castle, acquired

14

directly from Joseph Smith, "merchant-amateur" and British diplomat, as well as patron of the artist, who lived in Venice from 1710 to 1770. In the 153 Windsor drawings—which constitute nearly half of all the known pieces by Canaletto—the bright, crystalline atmosphere of Venice, sometimes veiled by a hazy glare, is vividly portrayed. After Rembrandt, nothing so rich and shining had been attempted in a drawing.

Recent publication of the entire Windsor series and the catalogue raisonné of Canaletto's drawings offered an opportunity to study the development of the artist's graphic style (Parker, 1958; Constable, 1962). But his training, still dubious for the paintings, appears even more vague for the drawings. We know that he began with stage designs, which tempts me to suggest a connection with Marco Ricci, who was active in the same field, also in the first decade of the century. At any rate, in Canaletto's early paintings, a romantic aura prevails, an interest which he shared with Ricci and which came from the same sources, namely, Roman landscape painting and Salvator Rosa. Also, when sketching his documentary views in Rome, Canaletto could have observed Pannini. These speculations seem confirmed by his early drawings, with their spirited, almost whimsical lines—between Rosa and Callot—and their vigorous, broad strokes, which often create chiaroscuro effects.

In his best Venetian period (1730–40) I believe that Canaletto enhanced the luminous and three-dimensional qualities of his drawings due to his experience with etching, but perhaps sacrificed some immediacy and romantic spark. Subsequently, in his English period (1746–53), while his paintings become increasingly disciplined—under the inspiration of Flemish or Dutch landscapes—the drawings grow more and more abbreviated and finally are a kind of brilliant shorthand for what they symbolize: the figures, the gondolas along the canals, dogs romping across the pavement, the curling clouds, and the choppy waves in the lagoon. But we can never accuse Canaletto of mechanical repetition or haste, because every work possesses his special poetic quality.

The drawings of his nephew, *Bernardo Bellotto* (1720–80) are not as exciting. They often resemble Canaletto's style but can be distinguished by a sharper, sometimes wavering, more realistic stroke. This is understandable when we consider that Bellotto, during his Dresden and Warsaw periods, was a great etcher. The majority of his drawings are preserved in the Dresden and Warsaw museums.

Francesco Guardi (1712–93) has left a significant number of drawings of all types and quality. Only a small quantity were published during the first quarter of this century (Damerini, 1912; Fiocco, 1923), but recently we have been able to arrive at an organic consideration of Francesco Guardi's graphic oeuvre. The main steps that led to this were the catalogues of the Correr (housing the richest group of Francesco's work—nearly one hundred and fifty items—not to mention many more by Giacomo) and of other collections such as the Uffizi and Horne Museum in Florence, the British Museum, the Metropolitan, the Ashmolean, the Albertina, and Berlin (Pallucchini, 1943; Arslan, 1944; Byam Shaw, 1951).

Distinguishing between the styles of the figure painter Gian Antonio Guardi and of his brother, the view painter Francesco, when he drew historical or religious compositions has been one of the achievements of modern criticism. This distinction must be the basis for the catalogues of each of the two painters (Morassi, 1953; Pignatti, 1957). Recently a subtle analysis of drawings previously attributed to Francesco has on the one hand eliminated consideration of his mysterious brother Niccolò as a draftsman and on the other shown how much Francesco was imitated by his son, the humble Giacomo (Pallucchini, 1949; Ragghianti, 1953; Pignatti, 1958 and 1963).

When works by members of his family and other followers have been correctly identified as secondary material, the oeuvre of Francesco Guardi remains a choice of masterpieces. He can easily be counted among the greatest draftsmen who ever existed. Graphic ideas expand in his drawings with a rapidity of touch that remains absolutely unique, revealing an inspiration that ranges from Callot's figures to Magnasco. At the same time, Guardi recreates the vital atmosphere of Venice in a setting that appears freely open to all our senses, in a space that is full of air and flickering light.

As for his subject matter, Guardi recalls the *vedutisti* of his time; he became the true heir of Canaletto when the latter left for his long stay in England. But Guardi surpasses both his matter-of-fact ideals and spirited Rococo décor; in his freest works he foreshadows Impressionism. His stylistic development is readily apparent and can be traced from the positive manner of his early compositions, large works showing the influence of Canaletto, to his late style, characterized by a glittering touch, especially visible in the Correr drawings (Byam Shaw, 1951).

The quality of Francesco's work stands out in contrast to the output of his followers and imitators, among whom only *Giacomo Guardi* (1764–1835) deserves mention. Giacomo fakes his father's style recklessly in pen drawings made for sale to foreigners, but found his true profession in painting precious tempera handmade "postcards," sold at his shop *al ponte del Peruchier* (at the hairdresser's bridge) in the early decades of the nineteenth century.

In this survey of eighteenth-century Venetian draftsmanship, *Gian Battista Tiepolo* (1696–1770) deserves special attention. His drawing activity has often been examined in important studies, but a catalogue raisonné—an arduous undertaking—is still wanting (Sack, 1910; Hadeln, 1927; Vigni, 1942; Lorenzetti, 1946; Pignatti, 1951; Knox, 1960).

In order to understand the problems connected with Tiepolo's drawings, we must first realize that his working methods were subject to regulation by the large family workshop. The Tiepolos operated in great accord, which makes it extremely difficult to separate the art of Gian Battista from that of his two sons, *Gian Domenico* (1727–1805) and *Lorenzo* (1736–76), and his closest assistants and followers, like Raggi, Ligari, Menescardi, and Zugno.

The workshop procedure in painting large frescoes began with creative sketches by Gian Battista and then continued through numerous series of detail studies executed by other members of the family. These typical sheets, mainly done in black or red chalk on blue-gray paper, were bound in original sketchbooks, like the three in Würzburg, one at the Correr, and one in Stuttgart; in addition there exist loose sheets in the Hermitage and others formerly in the Wendland collection, Lugano.

The attribution of the majority of these drawings to Gian Battista has not been doubted for some time, but now the question has arisen as to whether there are among them some by the sons or other members of the workshop (Vigni, 1956 and 1960; Seilern, 1958; Pignatti, 1961; Byam Shaw, 1962). Certainly the classifying method, which has been followed until now, of attributing a drawing to the author of the corresponding painting, is valuable but not totally reliable, considering the special working process of this family. The Tiepolos used to make preparatory sketches, but often they imitated existing works, which might have been made by different artists. In a large Gian Battista Tiepolo fresco there are often parts (heads, hands, draperies, decorative details) that obviously should be credited to Domenico or other assistants, and this involves the attribution of corresponding drawings. Finally, we must consider that Lorenzo often made prints after paintings and even drawings by his father. At the same time, some drawings—more or less of the "sketchbook type"—evidently originated from his activity as a printmaker. Obviously, it is not difficult to become almost hopelessly confused. Firm attributions can be made only when it is possible to check documentary evidence against style, working with unquestionable pieces, possibly made in more than one version by different members of the family. This happens, for instance, with some works in the Museo Bardini, Florence (corresponding to originals by Gian Battista in Trieste) and in Würzburg (originals at the Victoria and Albert; Seilern, 1959; Knox, 1960).

Trying to give a system for correct attributions of Tiepolesque drawings, I would say that Gian Battista's hand is always the most authoritative and creative, with fluid, wavy lines that swell subtly with the pressure of his hand. Domenico's style is usually slender and wavering, sometimes flickering, often reworked; his line appears uniform, even when he uses chalk or light pastel-pencil. Finally, Lorenzo is rather rudimentary, too insistent in shading, and more interested in an etching manner, as clearly shown in recent publications (Pignatti, 1951; Seilern, 1959).

With pen drawings, the situation is far clearer; in fact, I would say that an attributive problem does not even exist, owing to Gian Battista's outstanding personality. The most important pen drawings—nearly one thousand pieces—come from the unbinding of nine original albums bought in Venice in the early nineteenth century by Edward Cheney. The largest groups are now in the Victoria and Albert Museum (Cheney), the Morgan Library (Fairfax Murray), Metropolitan Museum (Biron), Princeton Museum (Platt), the Fogg Museum (Cheney, Orloff), Trieste Museum (Sartorio), Horne Museum, Florence (Horne), and the Albertina, as well as in the private collections of Count Seilern (Cheney, Orloff), Paul Wallraf (Cheney, Valmarana), and the duc de Talleyrand (Orloff).

The attribution of caricatures is still problematic. It is not too difficult, however, to distinguish Gian Battista's caricatures from Domenico's, after a careful study of signed drawings by the latter, which look humorous and exciting even though the lines are usually dry and uniform, drawn in chalky, dim light.

After we have solved most of the problems of attribution, Gian Battista's stature as a draftsman emerges with great clarity. He records on paper some of the happiest and most penetrating interpretations of life in the settecento. Like a new Paolo Veronese, he recreates all the spirited fervor and superb glory of the last great century of Venice. His brilliant drawings reveal an eager enjoyment of a social milieu in which moral scruples had totally vanished, whose aristocracy flourished vainly amidst decadence and golden ruins, while revolutionary ideas filtered in from France and the growing class of commoners.

The style of Gian Battista's late Spanish period shows marked changes from his early manner of the twenties. In his first works, he had still to overcome the academic traditions of his predecessors, such as Bencovich or Piazzetta. Sebastiano Ricci, too, played a great part in Tiepolo's education as a link between the styles of Barocci and the Carracci, and later, after his travels in the North, with Rubens. These were probably the ideals that originally led Tiepolo to the study of plastic modeling and light effects derived from strong contrasts. These influences are evident in his early black or red chalk sketches with white highlights and his pen and wash drawings. But soon he develops his own style, retaining the best of Venetian traditions but at the same time reflecting new foreign influences, mainly, I believe, that of Rembrandt. His acquaintance with the work of the greatest of all draftsmen was probably by means of drawings and prints, or perhaps through Pellegrini, when the latter first came back to Venice from the Low Countries. In addition, he must have known the Rembrandt-esque painters active in Venice, from Ghislandi to Bartolomeo Nazzari. In my opinion the luminous power of Tiepolo's drawings derives essentially from Rembrandt. This is particularly evident in works of the seventeen-thirties and forties, years that were most important in the full development of Tiepolo's style. Secondary influences of the same nature might have come from the lively etchings of the seventeenth-century painter Giulio Carpioni and some pieces by Guercino, in which the lines stand out in strong contrast against areas of blank paper.

In his late period, Tiepolo came under the influence of his son Domenico and re-

18

laxed his dazzling clarity in favor of lower-keyed harmony and more delicate shades.

The independent manner of Domenico after his father's death appears especially in illustrative drawings, marked by a characteristic humor, and a tendency to satirize social subjects. He lacks, however, true political sensitivity, and we cannot seriously maintain that he has an affinity to Hogarth or Goya. Like many transitional artists, Domenico was unfortunate in living too long. His last efforts were spent in caricaturing the Olympic patrician world, where he had lived and grown up with his great father (Byam Shaw, 1962).

At the end of the eighteenth century, all the great artists except for Domenico had disappeared from the scene. Remaining were such artists as *Pier Antonio Novelli* (1729–1804), perhaps a finer draftsman than a painter, with a style that is fluent and crisp like an etcher's; or more professional etchers such as Pier Antonio's son, *Francesco Novelli* (1767–1836), *Francesco Bartolozzi* (1728–1815), and *Antonio Zucchi* (1726–95). Last, and probably least in the "great tradition," is the eclectic, *Bernardino Bison* (1762–1844), an imitator of Guardi, Canaletto, Tiepolo, and Novelli, who has been greatly revalued in recent publications. Many works by these last-mentioned draftsmen show signs of being from a more modern period. The myths from which the Venetian settecento had drawn its own extraordinary story were dead.

Considering the importance of this century in the history of art, nobody would question the appropriateness of a special exhibition of Venetian drawings of the eighteenth century. We think it a great opportunity to bring such a show to the United States, where these drawings are fairly well-known and collected. This is practically the first time such an enterprise has been undertaken, and it is a great event not only for the general public that has long been so interested in Venetian art, but also for collectors and scholars.

This was surely the thought that spurred the Correr Administration and the City of Venice to grant an unusual loan of 120 of their best drawings for a traveling exhibition. The Correr Exhibition is a true homage by Venice to the multitude of lovers of her art, and, we hope, something more than a promise to settecento research.

It is difficult to believe that the drawing collection of the Correr Museum in Venice, one of the most important in the world, is at the same time one of the least known. Until now, it has been studied by only a few specialists on the basis of its fine groups of drawings by famous artists—such as the Guardis, Tiepolos, and Longhis—which have been included in exhibitions and recent books. In actual fact, the Correr ought to base its reputation just as much on a thousand other drawings by less famous artists. Taken as a whole, the collection provides a thorough and representative picture of Venetian eighteenth-century draftsmanship. In this comprehensiveness lies the ultimate value of our collection. It can rightly be called a research collection, thanks to its endowment of works by both the great artists and the many minor masters of the period.

The special nature of the Correr's collection of drawings is comparable to its collection of paintings, of which the first catalogue was published in 1960. Here too the lesser-known artists are well represented. The reason for this is the exceptional character of the Museum, determined by the personal taste of Teodoro Correr and the accession of many big collections formed during the eclectic period of the nineteenth century in Venice.

While the original estates of the patrician families of the *Serenissima* were being dissolved to overcome the financial difficulties of the new era, Correr, Molin, and Cicogna were acquiring heterogeneous collections of drawings whose importance was not then recognized. These were to become the foundation of our singular collection. The acquisition of the Guardi and Longhi series, from the painters themselves or from their immediate heirs, is certainly due to Correr. We still have Giacomo Guardi's receipt of October 26, 1829, for the sale of eighteen drawings by his father, Francesco, for the paltry sum of 14.5 lire. And we know that Nicoletto Guardi, Francesco's grandnephew, said in 1853 that all the drawings were in Giacomo's hands, and that he had been offered 200 zecchini for them but had asked 300. It must have been through Giacomo that the Guardis came into the hands of our founder, Teodoro Correr (Simonson, 1904; Pallucchini, 1943).

Nearly the same story can be repeated for the 140 sketches by Pietro Longhi, which Correr acquired from the painter's son Alessandro, as is stated in the first Museum Catalogue (Lazari, 1859). Correr probably also bought a group of more than one hundred drawings by the Tiepolo workshop, hitherto unknown, which were discovered in the museum store-rooms; these are by Gian Battista, Domenico, Lorenzo, and some minor followers.

A large addition to the collection came in 1841 from the Gamba bequest of an album that contained precious sheets by Guardi, Ricci, Canaletto, Piazzetta, Zuccarelli, and Pittoni. The Zoppetti bequest followed in 1852, with drawings by Guardi, Maggiotto, Piazzetta; Cicogna, in 1865; Molin, in 1885 (but the collection dates back to 1813), with a superb series of nearly two hundred Dizianis and Simoninis; Gatteri, in 1885, with the famous Tiepolo sketchbook of eighty-seven pages, bound in 1770; and recent gifts, such as Cini's in 1934, with twenty-eight Fontebassos, and Mauroner's Carlevaris album in 1948.

All these gifts, bequests, and more recently, acquisitions, have given the collection an eighteenth-century Venetian character. Because of its unity, comprehensiveness, and the quality of its series by major artists, the Correr can rightly take its place among the leading collections of the world for the study of Venetian draftsmanship in the settecento: the Uffizi and the Horne Museum in Florence, Windsor Library, the British Museum, the Louvre, and the Hermitage. I would also include in this list the Accademia in Venice, the museums of

20

Berlin, Düsseldorf, Frankfurt, and Stockholm, the Victoria and Albert Museum, the Ashmolean in Oxford; and American collections as well, such as the museums of Harvard and Princeton, the Morgan Library and the Metropolitan; and finally, private but well-known collections, such as those of Janos Scholz, Paul Wallraf, Count Seilern, Antonio Morassi, and the duc de Talleyrand.

A word of explanation about the collections of the municipal museums in Venice, from which the material of this show comes, would perhaps be helpful. Today the Musei Civici Veneziani are a complex of institutions with several subdivisions that includes in its holdings the original collections of Teodoro Correr—which give the popular name to the Museum—and subsequent acquisitions. The works of art are housed at the Procuratie Nuove in St. Mark's Square (history, renaissance paintings and sculpture, and art library); the Cà Rezzonico on the Grand Canal (seventeenth- and eighteenth-century art); and the Glass Museum, Murano.

So vast are the collections that interest in the drawings has been limited until now. Nevertheless, there are nearly nine thousand drawings (one half of them nineteenth-century architectural studies) now kept in the art library. Together with the rich collections of Venetian prints and illuminated manuscripts, they form an excellent "Prints and Drawings Cabinet." The majority of the choice drawings are from the Venetian settecento. This, at one and the same time, is both our limitation and our strength.

TERISIO PIGNATTI

Bibliographical References

ALBERTON, L. Novità su Egidio dall'Oglio. *Arte Veneta* (1962), pp. 183–185.

ALGAROTTI, F. *Il Newtonianismo per le dame.* Naples: 1737.

ARNOLDS, G. Das Venezianische Skizzenbuch von Canaletto. *Zeitschrift f. Kunstgeschichte* (1959), Vol. I, p. 57.

ARSLAN, W. Per la definizione dell'Arte di F., G. A., e N. Guardi. *Emporium* (1944), Vol. C, pp. 3–28.

BASSI–RATHGEB, R. *Un album inedito di Francesco Zuccarelli.* Bergamo: 1948.

BEAN, J. *Les dessins italiens de la collection Bonnat.* Paris: 1960.

——. Form and Function in Italian Drawings. *The Metropolitan Museum of Art Bulletin* (March 1963), pp. 225–236.

BELL, C. F. *Drawings by the Old Masters in The Library of Christ Church, Oxford*, Oxford: 1914.

BENESCH, O. *Venetian Drawings of the Eighteenth Century in America.* New York: 1947.

——. Marginalien zur Tiepolo Ausstellung . . . *Alte und Neue Kunst* (1952), pp. 53–69.

——. *Disegni veneti dell'Albertina di Vienna.* Venice: 1961.

BERTINI, A. *I disegni italiani della Biblioteca Reale di Torino.* Rome: 1958.

BETTAGNO, A. *Disegni e dipinti di Giovanni Antonio Pellegrini.* Venice: 1959.

BJURSTROEM, P. *Konstens Venedig-Teckningar.* Stockholm: 1962.

BLUNT, A. Paintings by Sebastiano and Marco Ricci in the Royal Collections. *The Burlington Magazine* (1946), pp. 262–268.

BLUNT, A., and CROFT–MURRAY, E. *Venetian drawings of the XVII & XVIII Centuries . . . at Windsor Castle.* London: 1957.

BYAM SHAW, J. Some Venetian Draughtsmen of the Eighteenth Century. *Old Master Drawings* (March 1933), pp. 47–63.

——. *The drawings of Francesco Guardi.* London: 1951.

——. The drawings of Francesco Fontebasso. *Arte Veneta* (1954), pp. 317–325.

——. *The drawings of Domenico Tiepolo.* London: 1962.

CAILLEUX, J. *Tiepolo et Guardi* . . . Paris: 1952.

CARLEVARIS, L. *Le fabbriche e vedute di Venetia.* Venice: 1703.

CLARKE, L., Jr. *Francesco Guardi.* Springfield: 1937.

COGGIOLA PITTONI, L. *G. B. Pittoni.* Florence: 1921.

——. Opere inedite di G. B. Pittoni. *Dedalo* (1928), pp. 671–695.

——. Disegni inediti di G. B. Pittoni. *Rivista di Venezia* (1934), pp. 263–289.

COLETTI, L. Nuovi affreschi di Gaspare Diziani. *Bollettino d'Arte* (1935), pp. 525–539.

Collection J. P. Morgan, Drawings by the Old Masters, formed by C. Fairfax Murray. London: 1905–12.

CONSTABLE, W. G. *Canaletto.* Oxford: 1962.

DA CANAL, V. *Vita di Gregorio Lazzarini* (1732). Venice: 1809.

DAMERINI, G. *L'Arte di F. Guardi.* Venice: 1912.

DELOGU, G. *Pittori minori veneti del Settecento.* Venice: 1930.

——. Disegni di Francesco Simonini a Venezia. *Dedalo* (1930–31), pp. 827–840.

DE MAFFEI, F. *Gian Antonio Guardi pittore di figura.* Verona: 1948.

VON DERSCHAU, J. *Sebastiano Ricci.* Heidelberg: 1922.

DOBROKLONSKY, M. V. Quelques feuilles inédites de Fontebasso aux Musées de Léningrad. *Arte Veneta* (1958), pp. 186–189.

——. *Ermitag-Risunki Italyanskay skoly 17–18 Vekov-Katalog.* Leningrad: 1961.

FENYÖ, I. Disegni veneziani nel Museo di Belle Arti di Budapest. *Acta Historiae Artium* (1959), no. 1–2, pp. 87–133.

——. Dessins Vénitiens du Settecento. *Acta Historiae Artium* (1960), no. 1–2, pp. 91–101.

FIOCCO, G. *Francesco Guardi*. Florence: 1923.

——. Le aggiunte di F. M. Tassis, *Rivista di Venezia* (1927), pp. 141–174.

——. La pittura veneziana alla Mostra del Settecento. *Rivista di Venezia* (1929), pp. 497–581.

——. *Giambattista Crosato*. Venice: 1941.

——. *Cento antichi disegni veneziani*. Venice: 1955.

FOGOLARI, G. *I disegni delle R. R. Gallerie dell'Accademia*. Milan: 1913.

VON FREEDEN, M., and LAMB, C. *Das Meisterwerk des Giovanni Battiata Tiepolo* . . . Munich: 1956.

FRITZSCHE, H. A. *Bernardo Belotto genannt Canaletto*. Burg b. M.: 1936.

GIOSEFFI, D. Per una datazione tardissima delle storie di Tobiolo . . . *Emporium* (1957), pp. 95–114.

——. *Canaletto–Il Quaderno delle Gallerie veneziane*. Trieste: 1959.

GOERING, M. Gian Battista Piazzetta als Zeichner. *Pantheon* (1941), pp. 259, 263.

——. *Francesco Guardi*. Vienna: 1944.

VON HADELN D. F. *Handzeichnungen von G. B. Tiepolo*. Florence: 1927.

——. *Die Zeichnungen von Antonio Canal, genannt Canaletto*. Vienna: 1930.

HASKELL, F. Francesco Guardi as Vedutista and His Patrons. *Journal of the Warburg and Courtauld Institutes* (1960), XXIII, no. 3–4, pp. 256–276.

HELD, J. S. *Great Master Drawings of Seven Centuries*. New York: 1959.

HETZER, T. *Die Fresken Tiepolos in der Würzburger Residenz*. Frankfurt: 1943.

Italian Drawings from the Janos Scholz Collection. Staten Island: 1961.

IVANOFF, N. Mattia Bortoloni e gli affreschi della villa Cornaro . . . *Arte Veneta* (1950), pp. 123–130.

——. Opere bergamesche di Mattia Bortoloni. *Emporium* (1957), pp. 7–13.

KNOX, G. *Catalogue of the Tiepolo Drawings in the Victoria and Albert Museum*. London: 1960.

LAFUENTE FERRARI, E. *Grabados y dibujos de Tiepolo*. Madrid: 1935.

LANCKORÓNSKA, M. *Die Venezianische Buchgraphik des XVIII Jahrhunderts*. Hamburg: 1950.

LAZAREFF, V. Francesco and G. A. Guardi. *The Burlington Magazine* (1934), LXV, pp. 53–72.

LEVEY, M. *Painting in XVIIIth-Century Venice*. London: 1959.

——. Domenico Tiepolo, his earliest activity and a monograph. *The Burlington Magazine* (1963), pp. 128–129.

LORENZETTI, G. I disegni di F. Fontebasso. *Rivista di Venezia* (1935), pp. 146–154.

——. *Cà Rezzonico*. Venice: 1936.

——. *Il Quaderno dei Tiepolo al Museo Correr di Venezia*. Venice: 1946.

LUGT, F. *Marques de Collections*. The Hague: 1956.

——. *Le dessin italien dans les collections Hollandaises*. Paris: 1962.

MAGAGNATO, L. *Disegni del Museo Civico di Bassano*. Venice: 1956.

MAURONER, F. *Luca Carlevaris*. Padua: 1945.

MIOTTI, T. *Il collezionista di disegni*. Venice: 1962.

MONGAN, A. *One Hundred Master Drawings*. Cambridge: 1949.

MONGAN, A., and SACHS, P. J. *Drawings in the Fogg Museum of Art*. Cambridge: 1946.

MORASSI, A. Un libro di disegni e due quadri di Sebastiano Ricci, *Cronache d'Arte* (1926), pp. 256–273.

——. *Disegni antichi dalla collezione Rasini in Milano*. Milan: 1937.

——. Settecento inedito: IV–Cinque teste di fantasia . . . *Arte Veneta* (1949), pp. 70–84.

——. A signed drawing by Antonio Guardi and the problem of the Guardi brothers. *The Burlington Magazine* (August, 1953), pp. 260–267.

——. *Dessins Vénitiens du Dixhuitième siècle de la Collection du Duc de Talleyrand*. Milan: 1958.

——. Pellegrini e Guardi. *Emporium* (November 1958), pp. 195–212.

——. *Disegni veneti del Settecento nella collezione di Paul Wallraf*. Venice: 1959.

——. *A Complete Catalogue of the Paintings of G. B. Tiepolo*. London: 1962.

MOSCHINI, V. *Francesco Guardi*. Milan: 1956.

——. *Pietro Longhi*. Milan: 1956.

Mostra Mercato Dell'Antiquariato. Florence: 1961.

MROZINSKA, M. *Disegni veneti in Polonia*. Venice: 1958.

MURARO, M. Novità su Francesco Guardi. *Arte Veneta* (1950), pp. 123–130.

——. *Mostra di disegni veneziani del Sei e Settecento*. Florence: 1953.

——. *Disegni veneti della collezione Janos Scholz*. Venice: 1957.

NEUMEYER, A. *Venetian Drawings 1600–1800*. San Francisco: 1960.

NICODEMI, G. G. *Piazzetta: 17 disegni inediti*. Milan: 1944.

OSTI, FRANCISCI. Sebastiano Ricci in Inghilterra. *Commentari* (1951), pp. 119–123.

——. In margine alla Mostra di Belluno: Marco Ricci. *Commentari* (1955), p. 32.

PALLUCCHINI, R. Il pittore Giuseppe Angeli. *Rivista di Venezia* (1931), pp. 421–430.

——. Antonio Marinetti detto il Chiozzotto. *Rivista di Venezia* (1932), pp. 27–34.

——. Francesco Daggiù detto il Cappella. *Rivista di Venezia* (1932), pp. 315–326.

——. Domenico Fedeli detto il Maggiotto. *Rivista di Venezia* (1932), pp. 485–495.

——. Federico Bencovich. *Rivista d'Arte* (1932), pp. 311–320.

——. Attorno al Piazzetta. *Rivista di Venezia* (1933), pp. 565–578.

——. *L'Arte di G. B. Piazzetta.* Bologna: 1934.

——. Profilo di Federico Bencovich. *Critica d'Arte* (1936), pp. 205–220.

——. Nuovo contributo al Bencovich. *Critica d'Arte* (1938), pp. 114–115.

——. Disegni sconosciuti del Piazzetta. *Critica d'Arte* (1938), pp. 152–154.

——. *Canaletto e Guardi.* Novara: 1941.

——. *I disegni del Guardi al Museo Correr di Venezia.* Venice: 1943.

——. *I disegni di Giambattista Pittoni.* Padua: 1945.

——. Nota per Gaspare Diziani. *Arte Veneta* (1948), pp. 135–138.

——. Nota per Giacomo Guardi. *Arte Veneta* (1949), p. 132.

——. Studi Ricceschi 2º: Contributo a Marco. *Arte Veneta* (1955), pp. 171–198.

——. Appunti per Giuseppe Diziani. *Arte Veneta* (1956), pp. 209–210.

——. *Piazzetta.* Milan: 1956.

——. Il Quaderno del Canaletto. *Arte Veneta* (1958), p. 236.

——. Altri disegni preparatori del Piazzetta. *Arte Veneta* (1959–60), pp. 220–222.

——. *La pittura veneziana del Settecento.* Florence-Rome: 1960.

PARKER, K. T. *The Drawings of Antonio Canaletto . . . at Windsor Castle.* London: 1948.

——. *Catalogue of the Collection of Drawings in the Ashmolean Museum.* Oxford: 1956.

——. *Disegni veneti di Oxford.* Venice: 1958.

PARKER, K. T., and BYAM SHAW, J. *Canaletto e Guardi.* Venice: 1962.

La Peinture Italienne au XVIIIᵉ Siècle. Paris, Petit Palais: 1961.

PIGNATTI, T. Disegni e incisioni. *Mostra del Tiepolo.* Venice: 1951, pp. 182–203.

——. Tiepolo incisore e disegnatore. *Fiera Letteraria* (1951), no. 24.

——. *Novità su Lorenzo Tiepolo.* Venice: 1951.

——. Venetian Seicento and Settecento Drawings. *The Burlington Magazine* (1954), p. 309.

——. Disegni inediti di Zuccarelli e Zais al Museo Correr. *Arte Veneta* (1956), pp. 177–182.

——. Drawings from the Museo Civico, Bassano. *The Burlington Magazine* (1956), pp. 373.

——. Nuovi disegni del Piazzetta. *Critica d'Arte* (1957), no. 23, p. 396.

——. Venetian drawings from the Scholz Collection. *The Burlington Magazine* (1957), pp. 385–386.

——. Un disegno di Antonio Guardi donato al Museo Correr. *Bollettino dei Musei Civici Veneziani* (1957), 1–2, pp. 21–32.

——. *Il quaderno di disegni del Canaletto alle Gallerie di Venezia.* Milan: 1958.

——. Il Ponte di Rialto del Palladio e un disegno guardesco del Correr. *Bollettino dei Musei Civici Veneziani* (1958), Vol. I, pp. 21–24.

——. Disegni Veneti del Seicento. *Mostra della Pittura Veneta del Seicento.* Venice: 1959, pp. 155–193.

——. Pellegrini drawings in Venice. *The Burlington Magazine* (1959), pp. 451–452.

——. Dipinti dal XVII al XVIII secolo. *Il Museo Correr di Venezia.* Venice: 1960.

——. Disegni di Tiepolo in Mostra negli Stati Uniti. *Arte Veneta* (1961), pp. 323–325.

——. Canaletto and Guardi at the Cini Foundation. *Master Drawings* (1963), no. I, pp. 49–53.

PILO, G. M. Otto nuove acqueforti ed altre aggiunte grafiche a Marco Ricci. *Arte Veneta* (1961), pp. 165–174.

PIPERATA, C. *G. B. Bison.* Padua: 1940.

PITTALUGA, M. *Acquafortisti veneziani del Settecento.* Florence: 1952.

POPHAM, A. E. *Italian drawings exhibited at the Royal Academy.* London: 1931.

RAGGHIANTI, C. L. *Epiloghi guardeschi.* Florence: 1953.

——. *Tiepolo: 150 disegni dei Musei di Trieste.* Florence: 1953.

——. Procedimento del Canaletto. *Selearte* (1959), no. 42, p. 33.

RAGGHIANTI-COLLOBI, L., and RAGGHIANTI, C. L. *Disegni dell'Accademia Carrara di Bergamo.* Venice: 1962.

RASMO, N. Recenti contributi a G. A. Guardi. *Cultura Atesina* (1955), pp. 150–160.

RAVA, A. *Marco Pitteri.* Florence: 1920.

——. *Pietro Longhi.* Florence: 1923.

RHODE ISLAND SCHOOL OF DESIGN, THE MUSEUM OF ART. *Italian Drawings.* Providence: March 27–April 16, 1961.

RIZZI, A. Il Grassi e i Guardi. *Emporium* (March 1962), pp. 99–110.

——. *Cento disegni del Bison*. Udine: 1962.

——. Guardi, Pietro Longhi e Tiepolo. *Emporium* (1962), pp. 155–164.

RIZZI, A. and GALLO, G. *Mostra di Nicola Grassi*. Udine: 1961.

ROSA, G. *Zuccarelli*. Milan: 1952.

ROSENBERG, J. *Great draughtsmen from Pisanello to Picasso*. Cambridge: 1959.

SACHS, P. J. *The Pocketbook of Great Drawings*. Washington: 1961.

SACK, E. *Giambattista und Domenico Tiepolo . . .* Hamburg: 1910.

SEILERN, A. *Italian Paintings and Drawings at 56 Princes Gate*, London: 1959.

Il Settecento Italiano, Catalogo della Mostra. Venice: 1929.

Il Settecento Italiano. Milan-Rome: 1932.

SCHOLZ, J. Notes on the drawings by F. Fontebasso. *L'Arte* (1948–51), pp. 40–42.

——. *Venetian Drawings*, Mills College. Oakland: 1960.

SINIBALDI, G. *Italian Drawings*. Washington: 1960–61.

STIX, A., and FRÖLICH–BUM, L. *Die Zeichnungen der Venezianischen Schule*. Vienna: 1926.

VALCANOVER, F. *Mostra di pitture del Settecento nel Bellunese*. Venice: 1954.

——. Affreschi sconosciuti di P. Longhi. *Paragone* (1956), pp. 21–26.

——. *La peinture italienne au XVIII siècle*, Petit Palais. Paris: 1960.

VIGNI, G. *Disegni del Tiepolo*. Padua: 1942.

——. Note sull'attività del Tiepolo a Madrid e a Würzburg e nel quaderno Correr. *Venezia e l'Europa*. Venice: 1956, pp. 363–365.

——. Tekeningen van Giambattista, Domenico en Lorenzo Tiepolo in Nederlande verzamelingen. *Bulletin Museum Boymans-van Beuningen* (1959), X, pp. 46–68.

VOLTOLINA, M. Pier Antonio Novelli. *Rivista di Venezia*. (1932), pp. 101–117.

——. P. A. Novelli illustratore di libri ed incisore. *Padua* (1933), pp. 28–38.

VOSS, H. Jacopo Amigoni. *Jahrbuch der Preussichen Kunstsammlungen* (1918) pp. 144–170.

WATSON, F. Some unpublished Canaletto drawings at London. *The Burlington Magazine* (1950), pp. 315–319.

——. Notes on Canaletto and His Engravers; Canaletto and Visentini. *The Burlington Magazine* (1950), pp. 291–293; 351–352.

WHITE, D. M., and SEWTER, A. C. Appunti su due disegni del Piazzetta al Museo Correr. *Bollettino dei Musei Civici Veneziani* (1962), no. 2, pp. 24–28.

Catalogue

Catalogue

Notes on the catalogue: The entries and reproductions are arranged in chronological order, and, for easy reference, an alphabetical index of artists follows the reproductions. In the catalogue entries, the number within parentheses that follows the title refers to the Correr collection number. Unless otherwise indicated, drawings are on white paper. Height precedes width in the measurements. Abbreviated bibliographic notes in the introduction and catalogue entries are fully given in the list of bibliographical references. One hundred out of the one hundred and twenty drawings are illustrated.

Sebastiano Ricci   1659 – 1736

1   THE CONTINENCE OF SCIPIO   (1774)
Pen and sepia and wash on yellowish paper. § 6¾ ×9¼ in.; 17.2 ×23.3 cm. § Inscriptions: *Scipione romano, Ricci* (in the artist's hand); *Scipione cede ad Alluccio Celtibero la sua prigioniera, Sebast. Rizzi fece* (in an eighteenth-century hand). § Provenance: Gamba, 1841; Museo Correr (Lugt, 1862a). § Literature: Pignatti, 1959, p. 192. § Exhibitions: Cà Pesaro, Venice, 1959, no. 102.

This striking sketch has been chosen to document Ricci's style at the beginning of the eighteenth century, when he painted many versions of this subject. A painting in Hampton Court is closely related to this sketch (Blunt, 1946, p. 267). Variations of the subject are now in Parma, Chatsworth, and the Palazzo Marucelli in Florence (1706). The mellow Giordanesque flavor of the drawing confirms Ricci's early experience in Naples.

2   FIGURE OF A WOMAN   (1741)
Black pencil and pen and sepia. § 3¾ ×3¼ in.; 9.5 ×9 cm. § Provenance: Gamba, 1841; Museo Correr (Lugt, 1862a).

This delicate, unpublished drawing is an example of Ricci's mature style and can be dated around 1725 because of its affinity to the Windsor sketch for the *Sta. Teresa* altar in Venice (Blunt, 1957, no. 334, pl. 35). It also seems to be related to figure studies recently acquired by the Metropolitan, by virtue of its quick and active pen lines drawn over transparent wash and pencil (Bean, 1963, p. 235).

Gian Antonio Pellegrini   1675 – 1741

3   THE JUDGMENT OF PARIS   (5508)
Pen and sepia and sepia wash. § 9¾ ×7½ in.; 25 ×19 cm. § Provenance: Molin, 1813; Museo Correr (Lugt, 1862a). § Literature: Bettagno, 1959, p. 73; Pignatti, 1959, p. 452; Valcanover, 1960, no. 349. § Exhibitions: Fondazione Cini, Venice, 1959, no. 105; Petit Palais, Paris, 1960, no. 349.

Traditionally this drawing has been ascribed to Diziani, but it must without doubt belong to the earlier Rococo period and, in particular, to Pellegrini. The appropriateness of this attribution is made obvious by the resemblance to Pellegrini's *Alexander and Darius* in the Hague Royal Cabinet, dated c. 1717–18.

4 VENUS TRIUMPHANT   (947)

Red pencil, pen and sepia, and sepia wash. § 9¼ ×7 in.; 23.5 ×17.8 cm. § Provenance: Correr, 1830 (Lugt, 461c, 1862a). § Literature: Bettagno, 1959, p. 52; Pignatti, 1959, p. 452. § Exhibitions: Fondazione Cini, Venice, 1959, no. 63.

Ascribed traditionally to Diziani, this drawing must be connected with Pellegrini, especially considering its affinity with the Düsseldorf *Allegory*, which could be its companion piece (Bettagno, 1959, no. 62).

Gian Antonio Guardi 1699 – 1761

5 MADONNA AND CHILD WITH THREE SAINTS

Red pencil, pen and brown ink, and brown wash on yellowish paper. § 14³⁄₁₆ ×8⅝ in.; 36 × 22 cm. § Provenance: Marius Paulme (Lugt, 1910); Antonio Morassi collection, Milan (loan 1963; Lugt, 143a). § Literature: Morassi, 1953, p. 261; Pignatti, 1957, p. 25; Byam Shaw, 1962, p. 48. § Exhibitions: Fondazione Cini, Venice, 1962, no. 53.

One of the masterpieces of Gian Antonio. Byam Shaw shares my opinion that this sketch is related to the *Belvedere di Grado* altarpiece, painted between 1746 and 1754. Some doubts are raised concerning the identification of the three saints, but they are probably SS. Domenico, Corbiniano, and Teresa.

6 FEBRUARY   (7040)

Black pencil, pen and gray ink, and gray wash. § 11¼ ×8¼ in.; 28.5 ×20.5 cm. § Inscriptions: *Febraro* (in the artist's hand); *Antonio Guardi Fecit. Anno 1760* (probably Francesco Guardi's hand). § Provenance: Carrer coll.; Morassi (gift 1950; Lugt, 143a); Museo Correr (Lugt, 1862a). § Literature: Fiocco, 1929, p. 571; Pallucchini, 1943, pp. 16, 41; Goering, 1944, p. 13; De Maffei, 1951, p. 55; Byam Shaw, 1951, p. 43; Morassi, 1953, p. 260; Pignatti, 1957, I–II, pp. 21–32. § Exhibitions: Settecento Italiano, Venice, 1929, no. 8.

This slight but interesting drawing has a great importance in the history of Gian Antonio Guardi's draftsmanship. The second inscription—very probably added after Antonio's death by his brother Francesco, as I suggested in 1957—is nevertheless a real clue to its authenticity. However, the word written in pencil, *Febraro*, is evidently by the same hand as the signature on sheets definitely identified as Antonio's.

In the sixties, after having completed his masterful screen for the organ loft at the church of Angelo Raffaele in Venice, Gian Antonio still had a light and vigorous touch. With perhaps some seventy known drawings, he should undoubtedly be placed among the greatest draftsmen of the early Rococo period (Pignatti, 1957, p. 21).

Nicola Grassi 1682 – 1748

7 CHRIST AT CALVARY   (5558)

Red and white chalk on brown paper. § 11¾ ×17¾ in.; 30 ×44.8 cm. § Provenance: Molin, 1813; Museo Correr (Lugt, 1862a). § Literature: Coggiola Pittoni, 1934, p. 264.

It seems likely that this drawing is by Nicola Grassi, an interesting provincial master who worked in the early eighteenth century and sometimes anticipated future evolutions of the Rococo. The close resemblance of this Christ to the one in Grassi's altarpiece in Endenna, *The Deposition*, dated 1731, supports this theory. The attribution to Grassi is surely more convincing than those of other drawings that have been given to him (Rizzi-Gallo, 1961, pl. 25). The similarity of this work, and especially of the summary sketch of the same subject on the *verso* to drawings by Pittoni is striking. Still, I would reject the attribution to Pittoni previously made by Coggiola Pittoni and ascribe this work tentatively to Grassi.

Federico Bencovich   *1677 – 1756*

8 MADONNA AND CHILD WITH TWO SAINTS   (5734)
   Black and white chalk heightened with white on brown paper. § 11 ×7⅟₁₆ in.; 27 ×18 cm. §
   Provenance: Molin, 1813; Museo Correr (Lugt, 1862a). § Literature: Pallucchini, 1932, p. 310;
   Pallucchini, 1936, p. 218; Muraro, 1953, p. 43.
Apparently among the latest drawings of the few certain ones by this artist. The influence of Tiepolo upon it was pointed out by Pallucchini when studying its connection with the *Holy Trinity* formerly in the possession of Dr. Sack in Hamburg, who considered the *Trinity* to be by Tiepolo (Sack, 1910, fig. 253). The Tiepolesque quality is characteristic of Bencovich's late style only, and therefore our drawing could be dated around 1740.

Gian Battista Pittoni   *1687 – 1767*

9 ALLEGORY OF FAME   (6067)
   Red pencil and wash on yellowish paper. § 6¾ ×3⅟₁₆ in; 17.1 ×7.8 cm. § Provenance: Fontana; Museo Correr (Lugt 461c, 1862a).
An unpublished drawing, related to other compositional sketches, such as Correr no. 1368 or no. 1365, although no such composition in oil is known (Pallucchini, 1945, p. 66, figs. 10 and 11). The wavy lines and painterly washes are reminiscent of Pittoni's best paintings around 1730. The *verso* shows a quick sketch of the same subject.

10 THE ADORATION OF THE SHEPHERDS   (784)
    Pencil heightened with white on brown paper. § 7⅛ ×3¾ in.; 18.2 ×9.7 cm. § See cat. no.
    11.

11 THE PRESENTATION OF JESUS IN THE TEMPLE   (786)
    Pencil heightened with white on brown paper. § 7½ ×3¾ in.; 19 ×9.6 cm. § Provenance:
    Correr, 1830 (Lugt, 1862a). § Literature: Pallucchini, 1945, p. 105.
These two *modelletti*, out of four at the Correr, are among the finest drawings by Pittoni and were evidently prepared as compositional models for presentation to a patron. One of the two not on exhibition, Correr no. 785, shows the Three Magi in approximately the same composition as the San Nazaro e Celso altarpiece in Brescia (1739–40). A study for the altarpiece, once in the possession of Count Barozzi, Venice, exhibits striking similarities to these *modelletti*, with their softly modeled areas and almost iridescent atmosphere (Coggiola Pittoni, 1934, p. 691).

12 THE INFANT JESUS   (7050)
    Red pencil. § 8⅟₁₆ ×5¾ in.; 20.5 ×14.4 cm. § Provenance: Correr, 1830 (Lugt, 1862a).
A preparatory sketch for an unknown painting, perhaps with a composition such as that of the *Adora-*

31

tion of the Shepherds, formerly in the Loeser collection in Florence (Coggiola Pittoni, 1921, fig. 6). A *Cupid* in a private collection in Padua, executed by Pittoni in the fifties, seems related, suggesting that our drawing dates from the same period (Pallucchini, 1945, p. 99, no. 116).

Jacopo Amigoni   1682 – 1752

13 PORTRAIT OF A GENTLEMAN   (737)
    Black chalk and gray wash. § 8¼ ×6½ in.; 21 ×16.7 cm. § Provenance: Correr, 1830 (Lugt, 1862a).

The Correr collection has two portrait drawings of this type, usually attributed to Amigoni's English period (1729–39). According to Janos Scholz, such drawings were bound together in a sketchbook, which went to the United States and was eventually taken apart (Muraro, 1957, p. 42). These typical drawings are not only in American collections, such as the Princeton University Museum, with five portraits, or the Scholz collection, but are also in the Stockholm Museum, the British Museum, and the Louvre. Dr. Bjurstroem, in his valuable Venetian Exhibition catalogue (Stockholm, 1962, p. 220) quotes Edward Croft-Murray, who seems to favor an attribution to the Englishman, Thomas Hudson. However, I still would prefer an attribution of the Correr drawing to Amigoni: its compositional idea, painterly style, and even the oval shape exemplify Amigoni's manner during the thirties.

14 HERCULES WITH MERIT AND GLORY   (1850)
    Red pencil, pen and sepia, and gray wash. § 11¼ ×7½ in.; 28.7 ×19.2 cm. § Provenance: Zoppetti, 1852; Museo Correr (Lugt, 1862a). § Inscriptions: *Rappresenta questo Soggetto, Ercole che tiene per mano il Merito presentato alla Gloria; simbolo degli onori e della Sapienza; con in lontano il tempio della Gloria, che riceve i suoi Eroi* (probably in the artist's hand); *Amigoni* (in a nineteenth-century hand).

An unpublished drawing, which can be attributed to Amigoni for evident iconographical and typological reasons; compare it, for example, to *Bacchus's Youth* in the Grauen Kloster, Berlin, or the *Prodigal Son* in Emmanuel College, Cambridge (dated c. 1734 by Pallucchini, 1960, p. 24). Subtlety and elegant draftsmanship are what we would expect of Amigoni's drawing style. At any rate, there are no better examples of his manner of composition; even the *Rebecca* in the Albertina (V. 318) is less convincing as an Amigoni drawing because of its surprising affinity to Bencovich's *S. Andrea*, also in the Albertina (engraved by Pitteri). Moreover, the attribution of the Correr drawing seems sustained by four related grisailles in the Graphische Sammlung and the Böhler collection in Munich (Voss, 1918, figs. 14–17). For its date, I would propose the forties, after the artist returned from England to Venice and before 1747, when he embarked for Spain.

Gian Battista Crosato   1685 – c. 1758

15 ZEPHIRUS AND FLORA   (960)
    Pen and black ink and sepia wash on gray paper. § 13¾ ×11 in.; 34.9 ×18 cm. § Provenance: Correr, 1830 (Lugt, 461c, 1862a).

An unquestionable addition to the few known drawings by Crosato. It can be easily compared to Seilern's *St. Charles Borromaeus*, no. 127 (first published by Fiocco, 1941, pl. 66) and to a ceiling sketch, given with certainty to Crosato because of Zanetti's valuable inscription (*ibid.*, pl. 70). This drawing must be placed in the period of the Stupinigi frescoes (1731–32); in fact, Zephirus resembles *Phaeton* in the Hunting Casino fresco, having the same curly hair and musculature. The foreshortening of the *putto* and the cornice with the giant vase is absolutely typical and appears in the Villa della Regina, Turin, in a painting dated 1733. Crosato's connections with Diziani and Fontebasso seem even more interesting after this identification.

Gaspare Diziani   1689 – 1767

16   THE FLIGHT INTO EGYPT   (5631)

Red chalk, pen and sepia, and gray wash on yellowish paper. § 8³⁄₁₆ ×16¼ in.; 20.8 ×41.2 cm. § Provenance: Molin, 1813; Museo Correr (Lugt, 1862a). § Literature: Derschau, 1922, p. 158, fig. 134; Coletti, 1935, p. 528; Fenyö, 1959, p. 91.

This is a preparatory sketch for the large canvas in St. Stephen's church sacristy, Venice. A *modelletto* is in a private collection in Bologna, but the drawing is closer to the painting, dated 1733. Comparing this drawing to earlier ones—such as *Mary and Elizabeth*, Correr no. 5518 (dated 1713 and executed in Belluno) or two studies of bearded heads, Correr nos. 5533–35 (inscribed *Dresda Polonia*, which dates them before his return to Venice in 1720)—Diziani's draftsmanship shows its evolution from late Baroque chiaroscuro washes in the manner of his teacher, Gregorio Lazzarini, through a hatching technique and a crispness influenced by Ricci, to a painterly Rococo style related to that of Pellegrini and G. A. Guardi. The medium is characteristic of his large preparatory drawings. The Molin Bequest, to which this sheet belongs, is the largest existing collection of Diziani's drawings. Nearly two hundred works, the majority bound in one volume, were collected by Ascanio Molin (1738–1813) during his lifetime. Their attribution to Diziani is especially convincing since Molin could have known the artist personally. Coletti has suggested that this album is the same that Da Canal mentions (1809, p. 36) as being in the possession of N. H. Zaccaria Sagredo. A second, similar album is now at the Albertina.

17   THE ASSUMPTION   (5645)

Pen and sepia on yellowish paper. § 15⁵⁄₁₆ ×11¼ in.; 39 ×28.5 cm. § Provenance: Molin, 1813; Museo Correr (Lugt, 1862a). § Literature: Valcanover, 1954, p. 92; Fenyö, 1959, p. 91.

Identified as the preparatory sketch for the *modelletto*, formerly in the Agosti collection and now in the Francesca Nicolis collection, Belluno. A different, perhaps earlier stage of this composition is shown in Correr no. 5627. The Madonna supported by angels appears again in the *S. Gervasio e Protasio* altarpiece at Belluno, although the lower portion of the painting is completely different. Pointing out compositional similarities to Sebastiano Ricci's *Assumption* in the Karlskirche in Vienna, Dr. Valcanover proposes a date around 1733, which seems probable.

18   ST. CECILIA AND A BISHOP   (956)

Black pencil and pen and sepia. § 11¹⁄₁₆ ×9¹⁄₁₆ in.; 28.2 ×23 cm. § Provenance: Correr, 1830 (Lugt, 1862a).

This unpublished drawing is unquestionably related to cat. no. 17. Forgetting the hatching for a moment, the contour lines of both works show absolute identity in style. Furthermore, from the standpoint of facial type, the bishop's profile is exactly the same as that of the second apostle from the left in cat. no. 17.

I am aware that a recent critical trend attributes the present drawing to Francesco Fontebasso. Dr. Fenyö also ascribes a number of other important works to Fontebasso, among them the Correr's *Minerva* (no. 5643), *Cherubs on the Clouds* (no. 5538), *The Assumption* (no. 5592), *The Coronation of the Virgin* (no. 5656); as well as the Albertina's *St. Bartholomew* (B. 346), *The Finding of Moses* (V. 327), and *Apollo and Marsyas* (V. 330); and Janos Scholz's *St. Christopher* (in spite of its typical Diziani sketch on the *verso*) and *Martyrdom of a Female Saint* (Fenyö, 1959, pp. 87–133, and 1960, pp. 91–101). However, I would still prefer attributing these works to Diziani. Regrettably, I am obliged to state my opinion of this complicated problem in a few words, contradicting my highly esteemed colleague with abridged arguments. The definition of Fontebasso's graphic style is limited to the concise, but well-grounded statement made by Dr. Benesch in his admirable book of 1947, p. 12: "His method of pen drawing, developing a tight net of modeling hatches, reveals the pupil of Ricci, who clung to the master's mode of shaping the solids." The *Nymphs*, in Princeton University, which Dr. Benesch reproduced in his book, is a perfect example of this hatching method. Moreover, that attribution was made by James Byam Shaw, to whom we owe the best article on the argument (1954, pp. 317–325). It is not by chance that the great English connoisseur, although familiar with all the Correr material, did not consider transferring any of the "hatched" Diziani drawings to Fontebasso. The pen drawings, from the Correr and other sources, that he gives to Fontebasso bear the distinct and characteristic etching net, with regular and parallel lines that rarely cross; a prototype is the signed piece entitled *Music* in the Ecole des Beaux Arts, Paris. Diziani's hatching, on the other hand, appears more painterly and irregular, suggesting color values.

As a final point, I add that one among the so-called Fontebasso drawings in the Correr, *Minerva* (no. 5643) looks like a study for one of the fresco *Allegories* painted by Diziani in the Spineda Palace, Treviso, about 1748.

19 THE ANNUNCIATION (5532)

Red pencil, pen and sepia, and sepia wash. § 16⅛ ×11⅜ in.; 41×29 cm. § Provenance: Molin, 1913; Museo Correr (Lugt, 461c, 1862a).

This unpublished drawing, with its shimmering light and spontaneity, is one of the finest works by Diziani. Considered to be a late drawing because of its connection with cat. no. 20, dated 1750, it reveals unexpected analogies to Pellegrini's style. In any event, the attribution to Diziani seems indisputable, especially after comparing it with a second version of the same subject (Correr no. 969) in which a more extensive use of wash creates a more painterly effect. Diziani repeated this subject in his *Annunciation* now in the Albertina (V. 238)—formerly attributed to Ricci and recently ascribed to Fontebasso (Benesch, 1961, p. 66, no. 96), following the methods of critical analysis mentioned previously in cat. no. 18. A painting by Diziani, dated in the fifties, has the same composition, but reversed; in 1961 it was acquired by the Belluno Museum from the Cramer Gallery (*Mostra dell'Antiquariato*, 1961, stand 29).

20 THE HOLY TRINITY AND DOMINICAN SAINTS (detail) (5573)

Black pencil, pen and sepia, and sepia wash. § 12¾ ×14¾ in.; 32.5×37.4 cm. § Provenance: Molin, 1813; Museo Correr (Lugt, 1862a).

The importance of this unpublished drawing lies in its connection with the fresco of 1750 in the church of S. Bartolomeo in Bergamo. An oil sketch for the fresco is in the Accademia Carrara. An-

34

other drawing in the Albertina (V. 326a) continues the composition of the Correr work. Interestingly enough, Diziani evidently pasted the Albertina sheet over the left-hand side of the present drawing so that the saint's cassock was completed and the arm below matched with a figure. In his last drawings, Diziani frequently used Pellegrini's device of exploiting blank areas of the paper.

21   THE FLIGHT INTO EGYPT   (5595)
      Black pencil and pen and sepia on yellowish paper. § 11⅝ ×8½ in.; 29.5 ×21.7 cm. § Provenance: Molin, 1813; Museo Correr (Lugt, 461c, 1862a).

This may be one of Diziani's last drawings, done in the sixties, when he seems to have been interested in the Tiepolos. This airy sketch possesses some of the crispness of Gian Battista's *capricci*, while the choice of subject matter may show the influence of Domenico Tiepolo's prints, issued in 1753.

22   TWO BISSONA COSTUMES   (5791)
      Black pencil, pen and sepia, and colored washes on yellowish paper. § 6¼ ×8⅝ in.; 15.8 ×22 cm. § Inscriptions: *Le Scienze n. 10 Barcaroli N. 6 Sonatori / Arti, n. 10 Barcaroli N. 6 Sonatori* (probably in the artist's hand); *Gasp. Diziani* (in a nineteenth-century hand). § Provenance: Vason; Museo Correr (Lugt, 1862a).

A charming, unpublished drawing (a second piece is at the Correr) with costume studies for two oarsmen, representing the sciences and the arts. They were evidently prepared for some carnival *bissone*, special boats used in festivals. Although no similar drawings by Diziani are known, this attribution is suggested by such a painting as the artist's *Festival of Sta. Marta* (Cà Rezzonico, no. 115), which also indicates an interest in genre subjects (Pignatti, 1960, p. 75). The date of the painting, around 1750, would be appropriate for the drawing.

Mattia Bortoloni   1695 – 1750

23   SUSANNAH   (5696)
      Black pencil, pen and gray ink, and wash. § 9⅞ ×8⅝ in.; 25 ×22 cm. § Inscriptions: *Bortoloni* (possibly in the artist's hand). § Provenance: Molin, 1813; Museo Correr (Lugt, 1862a).

This unpublished drawing can be attributed to Bortoloni on the basis of an Albertina drawing (Fiocco, 1927, p. 172, fig. 33). Some grisailles in the Villa Cornaro in Piombino Dese very closely resemble our drawing, which on this evidence might be dated around 1716 (Ivanoff, 1950, p. 130, fig. 145). In this sketch Bortoloni shows the influence of Ricci, while in later drawings he is said to have worked in a Tiepolesque manner. However, the only drawing in that style, the Bertarelli *Alexander*, is far from indisputable, even though it bears an old inscription (Ivanoff, 1957, p. 12).

Anton Maria Zanetti   1679 – 1767

24   THE EDUCATION OF ACHILLES   (1771)
      Black pencil, pen and sepia and gray ink, and sepia wash. § 8¹⁄₁₆ ×11⁷⁄₁₆ in.; 20.5 ×29 cm. § Provenance: Gamba, 1841; Museo Correr (Lugt, 1862a).

The attribution of this work, stated in old inventories, is based on comparison with a signed etching of the same subject by the artist. Zanetti's drawings often look clumsy, but in this drawing, as in the print, he tried to imitate Castiglione, who proved to be a good inspiration.

Gerolamo Brusaferro 1680 – 1760

25 A MIRACLE   (4309)

> Black pencil, pen and gray ink, and gray wash on yellowish paper. § 11 × 15 ½ in.; 28 × 39.5
> cm. § Provenance: Cicogna, 1865; Museo Correr (Lugt, 1862a).

Two drawings, one in the Albertina (V. 341) and the other belonging to Janos Scholz (Muraro, 1957,
p. 53, no. 87), bear the valuable attribution in A. M. Zanetti's hand to Brusaferro; a third drawing,
The Holy Family in Budapest (Fenyö, 1959, p. 126, fig. 54), bears a similar inscription in an eighteenth-
century hand. All three works resemble this unpublished sheet very closely. The present drawing,
which shows the artist's interest in Pellegrini, can be considered to be definitely by Brusaferro.

Gian Battista Marcuola 1711 – 80

26 THE VICTORY OF CYRUS   (5226)

> Red pencil, pen and sepia, and sepia wash. § 11¾ × 15 ⅝ in.; 29.8 × 39.8 cm. § Provenance:
> Bosa; Museo Correr (Lugt, 461c, 1862a).

In recent exhibitions we have often had an opportunity to see interesting works by G. B. Marcuola.
The signed drawings in the Hermitage (Dobroklonsky, 1961, pl. xcv) can be used as a guide to
further attributions. Because of obvious similarities to the Hermitage sheet, this sketch can be ascribed
to the same artist.

Francesco Fontebasso 1709 – 69

27 THE PRESENTATION OF THE VIRGIN   (5507)

> Pen and sepia, wash, and red ink. § 7 1/16 × 8 ⅝ in.; 18 × 22 cm. § Inscriptions: *Sebastian Ricci
> fecit* (in an eighteenth-century hand); *M.B.* § Provenance: Molin, 1813; Museo Correr (Lugt,
> 1862a). § Literature: Byam Shaw, 1954, p. 325.

A fine drawing with typical hatching, which is similar in technique and style to the *Design for a Wall
Decoration* in the Ashmolean Museum (no. 996). Byam Shaw dates the Oxford work around 1730,
noting an apparent Tiepolesque influence, which might possibly move the date up to the 1740's.

28 ST. JOSEPH WITH THE CHRIST CHILD   (1415)

> Black pencil and pen and sepia. § 8 1/16 × 7 9/16 in.; 20.5 × 19.3 cm. § Provenance: Zoppetti, 1852;
> Museo Correr (Lugt, 461c, 1862a). § Inscriptions: 7; *Fontebasso* (in a nineteenth-century hand).
> § Literature: Byam Shaw, 1954, p. 322; Fenyö, 1959, p. 113.

One of the few drawings done mostly in black pencil that can be attributed to Fontebasso. His training as an etcher is clearly apparent in the long parallel lines of hatching in this drawing. The work
also seems related to the so-called *Metastasio* in the Bassano Museum (Magagnato, 1956, p. 66, no. 70).

29 CHRIST AND THE WOMAN TAKEN IN ADULTERY   (6544)

> Black pencil, pen and sepia, and sepia wash heightened with white on yellowish paper. §
> 19¼ × 14 9/16 in.; 49 × 36 cm. § Provenance: Cini, 1934; Museo Correr (Lugt, 1862a). § Litera-
> ture: Lorenzetti, 1935, p. 146; Byam Shaw, 1954, pp. 319–320.

This is one of twenty-eight Biblical scenes in the Cini album. A second series of subjects from ancient
history has been identified by Byam Shaw, together with four works in the Albertina and others in

the Ashmolean, Courtauld, and Manning collections. These large drawings, all similar in technique, were probably made to be sold to collectors, which may account for certain weaknesses that appear in some of them. Then too, they may have been executed in haste, and possibly some of the work was done by assistants. This drawing is an excellent sheet, with brilliant lighting, refined lines, and a quality that is the sure sign of authenticity.

Bartolomeo Tarsia   1711–65

30   THE RAPE OF PROSERPINA   (245)
   Black pencil, pen and sepia, and tempera on yellowish paper. § 11⅜ ×15 in.; 29×38 cm. §
   Provenance: Correr, 1830 (Lugt, 1862a).

This is one of four *modelletti* in the Correr Museum, attributed to Tarsia on the basis of evidence in the old inventories. Dr. Salmina kindly informed me that they were made for the frescoes now at the Hermitage, where the painter worked in his late years. Tarsia has the qualities of a draftsman, close to Diziani's style, specifically in the use of iridescent glazes.

Jacopo Marieschi   1711–94

31   THE TRANSFER OF THE RELICS OF S. GIOVANNI ELEMOSINARIO FROM
      ALEXANDRIA TO VENICE   (1444)
   Black pencil, sepia, and tempera. § 6⅛ ×12⅛ in.; 15.5×30.8 cm. § Inscriptions: *J. Marieschi*
   (in an eighteenth-century hand). § Provenance: Zoppetti, 1852; Museo Correr (Lugt, 1862a).
   § Literature: Morassi, 1959, no. 43.

Marieschi was practically unknown as a draftsman, until Morassi discovered the lunette sketch of this same subject in the Wallraf collection and was able to identify it on the basis of the inscription on our piece. The present work is a *modelletto* for the lunette painted by Marieschi in S. Giovanni in Bragora in 1743. The Correr drawing is sketchier and more painterly than the Wallraf study, with many differences, especially in the background, from both the Wallraf work and the painting. Both drawings indicate that Marieschi was a follower of Ricci, as he uses the same fluid lines. Other obvious influences are the mid-seventeenth-century painters, notably the style of G. A. Guardi as shown in the *Fasti Morosini* in the Cini collection album.

Jacopo Guarana   1720–1808

32   AN ALLEGORY OF PANDORA   (970)
   Black pencil, pen and gray ink, and gray wash. § 13×8⅝ in.; 33×21.9 cm. § Provenance:
   Correr, 1830 (Lugt, 461c, 1862a).

So far, only tentative attributions have been made to Guarana. The *Diana* in the exhibition of Italian drawings from the Rhode Island School of Design, held in 1961, is quite likely by him (Catalogue, 1961, no. 93). This *Pandora* is in a similar style and is undoubtedly related to Guarana's fresco in the tapestry room of the Cà Rezzonico, painted about 1758 (Lorenzetti, 1936, p. 24), in which the falling figure in the foreground appears in an identical position. This similarity applies also to the flying cherubs, with rounded wings and long curly hair, and to the torch, represented in an unusual form that does not appear in work by other artists.

On the basis of these positive elements, I can propose this sketch to be an archetypal drawing for Guarana, who appears basically Ricciesque but also involved in the Venetian figurative culture of the fifties, represented by Diziani and Fontebasso. Guarana's compositional grandeur, which is always present, shows a firm background in the trend set by Ricci. This explains his great success as a decorator in Venice in the eighteenth century, especially the second half, when Tiepolo often worked abroad.

33 VENICE TRIUMPHANT (5665)

Black pencil, pen and sepia, and sepia wash on brownish paper. § 14×19¾ in.; 35.5×50.2 cm. § Provenance: Molin, 1813; Museo Correr (Lugt, 1862a).

With this drawing, formerly attributed to Diziani but here tentatively given to Guarana, we are trying to reconstruct Guarana's personality as a draftsman. The work is similar in style to the *Diana* at the Rhode Island School of Design (see cat. no. 32). Furthermore, its painterly handling resembles Guarana's *bozzetti*, such as the *Bacchus* in the Villa di Stra (Pallucchini, 1960, fig. 450) and the grisailles in the Cà Zenobio in Venice. The loosely formed lines correspond to the style of those paintings. Traits of Diziani's style can be easily explained, as they probably form one of the basic elements of Guarana's draftsmanship.

34 VENUS TRIUMPHANT (5473)

Brush and gray ink and tempera on yellowish paper. § 17 5/16×13 in.; 33×44 cm. § Provenance: Molin, 1813; Museo Correr (Lugt, 1862a).

A sketch for a ceiling decoration, which shows Guarana's typical muted colors and well-balanced compositions. The similarity to some *bozzetti* in the Villa di Stra (like *Time and Glory*, for instance) is startling.

35 MINERVA (968)

Black pencil, pen and black ink, and gray and reddish washes. § 11¼ ×7¾ in.; 29.5×19.8 cm. § Provenance: Correr, 1830 (Lugt, 461c; 1862a). § Literature: Fenyö, 1960, p. 96, fig. 3.

This drawing demonstrates the close contact between Guarana and Fontebasso, as has already been pointed out. Dr. Fenyö's attribution of this work to Fontebasso was based on a nineteenth-century inscription of a drawing of the same subject in Budapest (no. 2738), which is probably a sketch for the same painting (Fenyö, 1959, p. 109, figs. 29, 30). I have already discussed Dr. Fenyö's perhaps too generous concept of the number of definite works by Fontebasso (see cat. no. 18), and have reattributed some to Diziani. The same applies to the Budapest and Correr *Minervas*, which must be related not to Fontebasso but rather to the Guarana frescoes in the chapel of the Cà Zenobio, Venice, which have identical figures on the clouds, similar flying draperies, and the same technique of line and shading. We might date this work in the fifties (Pignatti, 1950, p. 145, note 1). These drawings all show close contact with Diziani, especially the *verso* of the Budapest sheet, in which Guarana used a painterly and nervous hatching.

Gian Battista Piazzetta   1683 – 1754

36 PORTRAIT OF A YOUNG MAN (1776)

Black and white chalk on brownish paper. § 13 5/8 ×11 3/16 in.; 34.6×28.4 cm. § Provenance: Correr, 1830 (Lugt, 1862a).

Even in his early years Piazzetta was famous for his drawings—made independently from his paintings—especially for the heads done in black and white chalk. Pallucchini quotes evidence for this from writings by Balestra, Anton Maria Zanetti, and other artists and amateurs from 1717 on (1956, p. 56). This portrait, hitherto unpublished, is a fine example of Piazzetta's style, probably of the seventeen-thirties. The characteristic highlighting resembles the *Boy and Girl with a Trap* in the Accademia (Pallucchini, 1956, fig. 157).

37 THE STANDARD BEARER   (7058)
> Black and white chalk on gray paper. § 20½ ×15⅝ in.; 52×39.8 cm. § Provenance: Correr, 1830 (Lugt, 461c, 1862a). § Literature: Pallucchini, 1934, pp. 58, 99, fig. 76.

One of the best large album drawings by Piazzetta, of the same subject as the Dresden painting. This work is later; I propose a date around 1740 because the same head with a large hat appears in the *Pastorale* in Chicago.

38 THE DRUMMER   (7057)
> Black and white chalk on gray paper. § 20½ ×15⅜ in.; 52×39.2 cm. § Provenance: Correr, 1830 (Lugt, 461c, 1862a). § Literature: Pallucchini, 1934, pp. 58, 99, fig. 75.

Pendant to cat. no. 37.

39 THE DEAD CHRIST AND FOUR SAINTS   (5682)
> Black pencil heightened with white on gray paper. § 14×8¼ in.; 35.5×21 cm. § Provenance: Molin, 1813 (Lugt, 1862a).

An unpublished drawing that can be attributed to Piazzetta on the basis of recent research on his compositional sketches. The upper part with a flying angel can be compared with the drawing of *San Vidal* in the Correr (Pignatti, 1957, p. 397, fig. 44), while the lower part with the saints is quite similar to the *Assumption* belonging to Janos Scholz, ascribed by Pallucchini to Piazzetta despite Zanetti's apparently erroneous attribution to Nicola Grassi. A new chapter in Piazzetta's drawings has been opened with such compositional sketches, which have a closer relationship than the chalk sheets to his extensive work as a book illustrator.

40 LADY AND NOBLEMAN IN CONVERSATION   (829)
> Red pencil. § 7¼ ×5³⁄₁₆ in.; 18.4×13.2 cm. § Provenance: Correr, 1830 (Lugt, 1862a).

In 1737, Count Francesco Algarotti, well-known collector-dealer and international connoisseur, issued his Newtonian dialogues, with a frontispiece that is probably a portrait of him talking with a lady (Ravà, 1920, p. 28, no. 280). The print bears the names of Piazzetta and Pitteri, designer and etcher, respectively. Two drawings, probably preparatory studies, of this subject are known, one in the Albertina (V. 279) and the other in the Kress Album, now in the Morgan Library. This drawing seems to be a counterproof of the Albertina study, probably made during the etching process.

Egidio dall'Oglio 1705 – 84

41 ST. JOSEPH AND THE CHRIST CHILD   (1643)
> Black and white chalk on gray paper. § 24⅜ ×19¹¹⁄₁₆ in.; 62×50 cm. § Provenance: Correr, 1830 (Lugt, 461c, 1862a). § Literature: Pallucchini, 1932, pp. 30, 34, fig. 7.

The problem of the correct attribution for sketches of heads in the style of Piazzetta is often a puzzling one, and I would like to be able to propose only positive attributions. Unfortunately, this is not yet possible. The drawing here illustrates my point. Up until now it has been attributed to Marinetti, but I believe that it might better be given to the oldest of Piazzetta's assistants, Egidio dall'Oglio. A large set of his original drawings, which Dr. Valcanover plans to publish, will confirm my attribution. Dall'Oglio's modeling is glazed and sharp, with an extensive use of white chalk for highlighting; this clearly distinguishes his style from that of his master. The same subject has also been drawn by Piazzetta himself in a similar sheet, now in the Alverà collection, Venice.

Domenico Maggiotto   1713 – 93

42 HEAD OF A PRIEST (1620)
Black chalk heightened with white on blue-gray paper. § 13¾ ×11¼ in.; 35 ×28.5 cm. §
Provenance: Correr, 1830 (Lugt, 1862a). § Literature: Pallucchini, 1932, pp. 492, 495, fig. 12.
A prototypal study by Maggiotto, which Pallucchini states corresponds to a detail in the painting *The Selling of Joseph*, now in the Metropolitan Museum (no. 29.70). The same subject appears in the *Icones ad vivum expressae*, engraved in 1754 by Cattini after works by Piazzetta, which explains the influence of the Piazzetta original. This drawing helps define the elements of Maggiotto's graphic style: characteristic exaggeration of highlights and shading, with angular contours and heavy finishing touches applied over the original lines.

43 A PEASANT GIRL IN PROFILE (1617)
Black chalk heightened with white on blue-gray paper. § 13⁹⁄₁₆ ×10¹³⁄₁₆ in.; 34.5 ×27.5 cm. §
Provenance: Correr, 1830 (Lugt, 1862a). § Literature: Pallucchini, 1932, pp. 492, 495, fig. 10.
Companion piece to cat. no. 42. It closely resembles a drawing at Windsor entitled *Girl in Contemplation*; the model looks exactly the same (Blunt, 1957, p. 29, no. 43). As the Windsor drawings are dated around the thirties, this might be one of the earliest works by Maggiotto, drawn from life, when he was a young assistant in Piazzetta's workshop.

44 STUDY OF A FEMALE NUDE (6987)
Black chalk heightened with white on gray paper. § 17¾ ×22⅞ in.; 45.1 ×57 cm. § Provenance: Donà dalle Rose, 1935; Museo Correr (Lugt, 1862a).
A sheet from an unpublished sketchbook now at the Correr, which was used by Piazzetta's pupils or assistants. We often find among these drawings some familiar types of models that have been copied many times. Many etchings in Pitteri's *Studi di Pittura*, issued in 1760 by Albrizzi in Venice, reproduce these academic models. Therefore, one may conclude that the pupils sat in the same room around the model, as was done in the *Accademia di Pittura*; this would explain the reason why we find drawings of the same model done from different angles by different artists, including the master (Albertina, Morassi, Alverà, Koenigs, Ashmolean, Modena Galleria Estense). I wish to ascribe this nude, one of the finest sheets in our sketchbook, to Maggiotto because of the clean shading and strong retouching. The comparison with the *Nude Woman* in the Estense Gallery, given to Piazzetta, speaks in favor of my attrition. It can be dated about 1750, when Piazzetta started teaching in the *Accademia di Pittura* at the Fonteghetto delle Farine (Pallucchini, 1938, p. 152, fig. 3).

Francesco Cappella   1714 – 84

45 A PEASANT GIRL (378)
Black and white chalk on gray paper. § 19³⁄₁₆ ×14⁹⁄₁₆ in.; 48.7 ×37 cm. § Provenance: Correr,

40

1830 (Lugt, 461c, 1862a). § Literature: Pallucchini, 1932, p. 324, fig. 13; *ibid.*, 1956, p. 50, fig. 116.

Correctly given to Cappella by Pallucchini in his first article on the artist, and subsequently transferred to Piazzetta. I still believe that the artist is Cappella, and this can be confirmed by some similar drawings in Bergamo. Because Cappella's paintings are very much like Piazzetta's, it is understandable that a similarity exists between their drawings as well.

Giuseppe Nogari   1699 – 1763

46 HEAD OF AN OLD WOMAN   (742)
    Black and red pencil heightened with white on gray paper. § 10⅞×6⅞ in.; 22.8×17.4 cm. §
    Provenance: Correr, 1830 (Lugt, 1862a).

An unpublished drawing by Nogari, who is much better known as a pastel painter than as a draftsman. The attribution relies on one of the few drawings known to be by the artist, the *Boy's Head* in the Estense Gallery in Modena (Pallucchini, 1933, p. 572, fig. 11). It is interesting to note that this head was discovered among the extensive Longhi collection in the Correr, which was acquired directly from Alessandro Longhi. In his early years, Alessandro was Nogari's pupil.

Pietro Longhi   1702 – 85

47 A PEASANT GIRL BROACHING A CASK   (523)
    Black pencil heightened with white on brown paper. § 17¼ ×11½ in.; 43.8×39.2 cm. §
    Provenance: Correr, 1830. § Literature: Moschini, 1956, fig. 207; Rizzi, 1962, p. 162, fig. 7;
    Bjurstroem, 1962, p. 230. § Exhibitions: National Museum, Stockholm, 1962, no. 304.

Most of Pietro Longhi's handsome drawings are related to paintings and were used by the artist for definite study purposes. Although many of these sheets, a majority of which are in the Correr, have been published in monographs on Longhi, the problem of chronology is still under discussion and is made more difficult by the peculiar uniformity of Longhi's style. However, this drawing can be dated around the 1740's as it is connected with the execution of a series of paintings of peasant life, some of which are now in the Cà Rezzonico in Venice and others in Zoppola Castle, near Udine (Rizzi, 1962, p. 162). Some slight variations have been made in the painting, especially in the male figure, which has been changed into an old man, but this often happens in Longhi's studies. The heavy chiaroscuro and the shading in order to model forms are typical of his early style and will gradually disappear in later works.

48 THE HAIRDRESSER   (441)
    Black pencil heightened with white on brown paper. § 10¹¹⁄₁₆ ×17⅛ in.; 27.7×43.5 cm. §
    Provenance: Correr, 1830 (Lugt, 1862a). § Literature: Valcanover, 1956, p. 25; Moschini, 1956,
    fig. 161.

This is a preparatory drawing for the painting at the Cà Rezzonico, Venice (no. 128), dated about 1760. The Doge in the portrait is not contemporary but an ancestor of the family, Carlo Ruzzini, who died in 1735.

49 A LADY SPINNING   (465)
    Black pencil heightened with white on brown paper. § 11 ×15⅛ in.; 28×38.5 cm. § Prove-

nance: Correr, 1830 (Lugt, 461d, 1862a). § Literature: Ravà, 1923, p. 139; Bjurstroem, 1962, p. 230. § Exhibitions: National Museum, Stockholm, 1962, no. 305.

No painting after this drawing is known, but one probably did exist originally. There is an etching by Flipart entitled *Avowal of Love*, which shows a lady spinning and is inscribed "Pietro Longhi pinxit." The print dates from before 1750. A painting after the print is in the Cà Rezzonico (no. 141). Both the print and the copy are in reverse of the present drawing.

50 A LADY FANNING A GENTLEMAN (454)

Black pencil heightened with white on brown paper. § 11 $\frac{7}{16}$ × 17 in.; 29 × 43.2 cm. § Provenance: Correr, 1830 (Lugt, 461d, 1862a). § Inscriptions: *letto; così fiancegiata Legiadra* (in the artist's hand). § Literature: Moschini, 1956, fig. 41.

A sketch that is full of life, with a notation about something "slender and pretty," probably the lady's waist. The drawing dates from the fifties and is similar to some studies at the Correr for *The Awakening*, at Windsor.

51 A LADY FEEDING HER CANARY (510)

Black pencil heightened with white on brown paper. § 11 $\frac{1}{4}$ × 13 $\frac{5}{16}$ in.; 28.5 × 33.8 cm. § Provenance: Correr, 1830 (Lugt, 461d, 1862a). § Literature: Ravà, 1923, p. 136.

The lady is standing on a stool to reach the cage. Atmosphere seems to fill the space around her. No painting related to this drawing is known.

52 A GENTLEMAN BOWING (491)

Black pencil heightened with white on brown paper. § 11 × 11 $\frac{13}{16}$ in.; 28 × 30 cm. § Provenance: Correr, 1830 (Lugt, 461d, 1862a). § Literature: Valcanover, 1956, p. 25; Moschini, 1956, fig. 153.

The drawing was used for the painting *Gentleman Joining a Party*, now in the Perera collection, New York (Moschini, 1956, fig. 156). Dr. Valcanover has suggested a date around 1761.

53 A GENTLEMAN SEATING A LADY

Black pencil heightened with white on brown paper § 11 × 14 $\frac{3}{8}$ in.; 28 × 36.6 cm. § Provenance: Correr, 1830 (Lugt, 461d, 1862a) § Literature: Ravà, 1923, p. 140; Paris Catalogue, 1960, no. 334 § Exhibitions: Petit Palais, Paris, 1960, no. 334.

A penetrating sketch from life. No painted version is known.

54 HUNTING IN THE LAGOON (475)

Black pencil heightened with white on brown paper. § 11 $\frac{1}{2}$ × 17 $\frac{3}{4}$ in.; 29.2 × 45 cm. § Provenance: Correr, 1830 (Lugt, 461d, 1862a). § Inscriptions: *La camisola qui; I zocheti* (in the artist's hand). § Literature: Ravà, 1923, p. 133; Valcanover, 1956, p. 25; Paris Catalogue, 1960, no. 338. § Exhibitions: Petit Palais, Paris, 1960, no. 338.

Most likely sketched on the spot, this drawing is a study for the painting now in the Querini Stampalia Gallery, Venice, and is dated around 1770 by Dr. Valcanover. At this time Longhi's style is marked by a trend towards freer lines and more summary forms, but the drawings retain their practical function as steps in his working process. The inscriptions, with notes on the white shirts of the boatmen and details of the boat, are additional guides to the artist's memory.

55 NURSE AND CHILD WITH A MIRROR FRAME (483)

Black pencil heightened with white on brown paper. § 11 $\frac{5}{8}$ × 17 $\frac{7}{16}$ in.; 29.5 × 48.3 cm. §

42

Provenance: Correr, 1830 (Lugt, 461d, 1862a). § Inscriptions: *d'oro; verde; più lungo; roseto; bianco; indiano manega bareta* (in the artist's hand). § Literature: Moschini, 1956, fig. 169; Paris Catalogue, 1960, no. 340. § Exhibitions: Petit Palais, Paris, 1960, no. 340.

One of our finest drawings. Preparatory study for *Family Portrait*, Salom collection, Venice.

Alessandro Longhi   1733 – 1813

56   FAMILY PORTRAIT   (577)
Black pencil, pen and sepia, and sepia wash. § 13⅞ ×16⅜ in.; 34.5 ×41.7 cm. § Provenance: Correr, 1830 (Lugt, 461c, 1862a). § Inscriptions: *Longhi* (in a nineteenth-century hand). § Literature: Byam Shaw, 1933, p. 60.

As a draftsman, Alessandro Longhi is practically unknown; only a few characteristics can be determined by studying his etchings, executed in 1761 for his *Vite dei pittori*. This drawing, part of the original Longhi group, is closely related to Alessandro's early paintings, such as the large *Pisani Family*, now in the Bentivoglio collection in Venice. Alessandro Longhi was commissioned in 1762 to paint two large portraits of the Pisani family, but only one is known today. I think it quite possible that this drawing is a study for the second Pisani painting. In the catalogue of Alessandro Longhi's drawings, this sketch seems related to Janos Scholz's *Portrait of a Gentleman* (Benesch, 1947, p. 36, no. 47).

57   PORTRAIT OF DOGE MOROSINI   (581)
Black pencil heightened with white on gray paper. § 10⁹⁄₁₆ ×8¼ in.; 26.9 ×20.5 cm. § Provenance: Correr, 1830 (Lugt, 461c, 1862a). § Inscriptions: *Francesco Morosini generalle della S.ma Repubblica conquistador della Morea, il suo corpo in S. Stefano* (possibly in the artist's hand).

From the diaries of Pietro Gradenigo, a Venetian of the eighteenth century, we know that Alessandro exhibited one of his first portraits in May 1757, and the painter himself informs us in his *Vite dei pittori* (issued in 1762) that his first master in portraiture was Giuseppe Nogari. Therefore, as this portrait from the Longhi group at the Correr so closely resembles Nogari's style, I have attributed it to Alessandro rather than to his father.

58   THE WINE CELLAR AT SAN MARCO'S   (584)
Black pencil heightened with white on brown paper. § 10¹³⁄₁₆ ×16⅝ in.; 27.5 ×42.2 cm. § Inscriptions: *1790; W S. Marcho W* (in the artist's hand). § Provenance: Correr, 1830 (Lugt, 461c, 1862a).

An unpublished drawing from the Longhi group. The inscribed date, 1790, does not permit attribution to Pietro, who died in 1785. The drawing seems to be by Alessandro, working in a manner surprisingly close to his father's late style. No painting of the subject is known.

Marco Ricci   1676 – 1729

59   LANDSCAPE WITH A MILL
Black pencil, pen and sepia, and sepia wash. § 10³⁄₁₆ ×15 in.; 25.8 ×38.1 cm. § Provenance: Italico Brass collection, Venice (loan 1963). § Literature: Pilo, 1961, p. 172, fig. 217.

One of the most vibrant drawings by Marco Ricci, executed in the manner of Domenico Campagnola. While Pallucchini places these drawings very early in Ricci's career (1955, p. 173), Blunt dates them in the artist's late period, when he did many etchings, from about 1723 onwards (1957, p. 39). Blunt further points out that all Ricci's drawings in this style at Windsor come from Smith's albums, which indicates a late date. The English consul was in touch with Marco Ricci only during the artist's last years after his return from England in 1716. Considering the open expanse of landscape bathed in soft light, as in some of Ricci's later paintings, I would join Blunt in calling this drawing —which corresponds to another one at Windsor (no. 98)—a late work.

60 LANDSCAPE WITH A BRIDGE   (5370)
   Black pencil, pen and sepia, and sepia wash. § 8¼ ×11¹³⁄₁₆ in.; 21.6×32 cm. § Provenance:
   Molin, 1813; Museo Correr (Lugt, 1862a).

A fine unpublished sheet by Ricci, in the style of the previous drawing. A quick sketch, this landscape shows an earlier stage in the development of an idea than other large and more finished drawings in the same manner.

61 STAGE DESIGN WITH FIGURES   (224)
   Black pencil, pen and sepia, and sepia wash on yellowish paper. § 12⅝ ×8⅝ in.; 32 ×22 cm. §
   Inscriptions: *Canaletto* (in a nineteenth-century hand). § Provenance: Correr, 1830 (Lugt,
   461d, 1862a).

This unpublished stage design is of the type that Marco Ricci did during his stay in England from 1708 to 1710. He collaborated there with Pellegrini on the settings for "Phyrrus," "Camilla," "Idaspe Fedele," and other operas. Many of these drawings are now at Windsor. Exact dating of his stage designs is rather difficult, for Ricci did this sort of work throughout his life (Blunt, 1957, p. 41). However, I would place this drawing close to no. 180 at Windsor, which is considered to be a bit later than the English works—in the second decade.

62 A SOLDIER   (1475)
   Pen and black ink. § 6×4⅛ in.; 15.3 ×10.5 cm. § Provenance: Correr, 1830 (Lugt, 1862a).
This unpublished drawing, which has a second soldier sketched on the *verso*, can be attributed to Marco Ricci on the basis of *The Pilgrim Family* in Princeton (Benesch, 1947, no. 3) and the signed work, *Three Men Near a Pyramid*, in the Fogg Museum (Mongan and Sachs, 1946, no. 345). In this early study, Marco's style is close to his uncle, Sebastiano, who often placed similar figures in his landscapes. A comparison of this drawing with a *Beggar* at Windsor (no. 400) is most interesting and raises questions concerning that attribution. Janos Scholz owns a drawing of this type, representing a guitar player (Scholz, 1960, no. 67).

Antonio Visentini 1688 – 1782

63 IMAGINARY LANDSCAPE WITH OBELISK   (1457)
   Brush and sepia wash, heightened with white. § 6⅞ ×9¼ in.; 17.5 ×23 cm. § Inscriptions:
   M. Ricci 18 (in an eighteenth-century hand). § Provenance: Zoppetti, 1852, Museo Correr
   (Lugt, 1862a).

The Windsor Library collection has many albums by Visentini, from Consul Smith and other sources. Some drawings among these are very close to the present landscape, permitting us to make a sure attribution. Two of the Windsor sheets, nos. 548 and 555, especially resemble the Correr

44

work in that each has been heightened with white, probably in order to give a more finished effect and make it more saleable.

Francesco Simonini   *1686 – 1753*

64 CAVALRY BATTLE   (5752)
   Black pencil, pen and sepia, and sepia wash. § 15⅜ ×26⅛ in.; 39 ×63.3 cm. § Inscriptions: *F.S.* (probably in the artist's hand). § Provenance: Molin, 1813; Museo Correr (Lugt, 1862a) § Literature: Delogu, 1930–31, p. 840.

The many drawings by Simonini at the Correr are executed in two different manners. The first is a sketchy one, with dense and dramatic brushwork, flashing highlights, and retouched contours; the second is more finished, done mainly in pen with lighter washes. This drawing, signed by the artist, is perhaps the best of the first group and could well be used as a guide for further attributions to this brilliant painter of battle scenes. Simonini worked as the personal documentary painter for the famous Marshal Schulemburg, a general of the Venetian army in the eighteenth century who was also an art collector.

Giuseppe Zais   *1709 – 84*

65 CAVALRY BATTLE   (4605)
   Brush and sepia wash and tempera. § 14⅝ ×20¾ in.; 37.1 ×52.7 cm. § Provenance: Correr, 1830 (Lugt, 1862a). § Literature: Pignatti, 1956, p. 181, fig. 198.

A number of recent publications have discussed Zais as a painter of battle scenes and his evident connection with Simonini. Most likely Zais met Simonini in Venice in the forties and showed an interest in his genre, for many of Zais's paintings and drawings of this subject are known. The present drawing is one of the most brilliant and shows the painter's tendency to use the bright colors of Casanova, also well known in Venice.

66 LANDSCAPE WITH WOMEN WASHING   (5769)
   Brush and sepia wash and tempera. § 15¾ ×21¼ in.; 40 ×54 cm. § Provenance: Molin, 1813; Museo Correr (Lugt, 1862a). § Literature: Delogu, 1930, p. 142; Pignatti, 1956, p. 182.

One of the large temperas from the Correr, in the usual manner of Zais's series for sale to collectors. In these colored drawings, probably executed after 1750, the contacts with Zuccarelli are more evident than before, notably in the shading and brightness of color (Pignatti, 1956, p. 181). They can easily be distinguished from Zuccarelli, however, by the crisp lines that show the influence of Ricci.

67 THE RAPE OF EUROPA   (5764)
   Pen and sepia, gray wash, and gray ink. § 10¹¹⁄₁₆ ×16½ in.; 21.2 ×32 cm. § Provenance: Molin, 1813; Museo Correr (Lugt, 1862a). § Literature: Delogu, 1930, p. 142; Pignatti, 1956, p. 179, fig. 194.

Two drawings at the Correr depict the legend of Europa; this, with its painterly washes in the shading, is the more finished of the two. The subject probably comes from Zuccarelli, who painted Europa many times (Gallerie dell'Accademia, Venice), but Zais gives his own interpretation with crisp lines and vibrant light, which suggest the sharp and dazzling colors of his paintings.

Francesco Zuccarelli   1702 – 88

68   LANDSCAPE WITH PEASANTS   (5379)
Pen and sepia, brush and sepia wash and colored washes on yellowish paper. § 8 ⅝ × 14 ⅜ in.;
22 × 36 cm. § Provenance: Molin, 1813; Museo Correr (Lugt, 1862a). § Literature: Pignatti,
1956, p. 178, fig. 192. § Exhibitions: Washington, D. C., 1960, no. 139.

Although at the outset Zuccarelli did not appear to have the makings of a great draftsman, he has
left a large number of excellent drawings. From pencil or pen studies to large album sheets, we can
always find a genuine painterly quality, which makes his drawings quite close in style to his paintings.
The present drawing has been badly cut at the edges, but we can still admire the immediacy of its
color effects, which have been achieved with characteristic washes over the pen drawing. I would
suggest a date in the fifties, because of similarities to drawings in the Tassi album (Bassi-Rathgeb,
1948).

69   LANDSCAPE WITH SHEPHERDESS
Black chalk on yellowish paper. § 10 ⅞₆ × 14 ⅞ in.; 26.5 × 37.8 cm. § Inscription: *F. Zuccarelli
f.* (in an eighteenth-century hand). § Provenance: Antonio Morassi collection, Milan (loan
1963; Lugt 143a). § Literature: Rosa, 1952, p. 8. § Exhibitions: Lausanne, 1947, no. 174.

A fine example of Zuccarelli's mature pencil drawings. In style and iconography; the figures might
recall some typical subject of the fifties or even sixties, like the pastorals from Carrara, Bergamo, or
the Grassi collection in New York (Pallucchini, 1960, fig. 514).

Luca Carlevaris   1663 – 1730

70   PALAZZO LABIA AND TWO SKETCHES OF A GENTLEMAN   (6962)
Black pencil on yellowish paper. § 8¼ × 11¾ in.; 20.5 × 30 cm. § Inscriptions: Numbers in
the artist's hand. § Provenance: Mauroner, 1948; Museo Correr (Lugt, 1862a). § Literature:
Mauroner, 1945, p. 70.

This is one of the most interesting sheets from the Mauroner album, a miscellaneous series of drawings in pen and pencil, showing architecture, figures, and caricatures, pasted on twenty-nine sheets.
It is interesting to note that one page has a hole in it out of which a drawing of a gondola was cut.
(We owe this information to Janos Scholz, who now owns the drawing, reproduced by Muraro,
1957, no. 77.) The profile on the left of the Correr work might be a portrait of Sebastiano Ricci, as
he appears in paintings and in Marco Ricci's caricature at Windsor (Blunt, 1957, fig. 18, no. 2). This
evidence suggests a date of about 1730. The gentleman at the right appears to be earlier, judging by
the costume with a typical long wig and large *velada* coat—around 1710–20. The architectural study
in the middle is of the Palazzo Labia, whose façade on the Rio di Cannaregio was built by Cominelli
—before 1703, for it is illustrated in Carlevaris's book of prints, *Le Fabbriche e Vedute di Venezia*,
issued in that year. This drawing was probably used for the etching.

71   LAGOON WITH TWO BOATS   (5949)
Pen and sepia and sepia wash, heightened with white on gray paper. § 8¾ × 7¹³⁄₁₆ in.; 22.2 ×
19.9 cm. § Provenance: Corniani Algarotti collection, 1893; Museo Correr (Lugt, 1862a). §
Literature: Mauroner, 1945, p. 69, fig. 44.

46

A typical example of Carlevaris's drawings from an album of twenty-four pages that contains nine-teenth-century inscriptions, referring to previous ownership by Count Corniani Algarotti, Venice.

Antonio Canal, called Canaletto   1697 – 1768

72 FOUR ARCHITECTURAL SKETCHES (1785)

Pen and sepia. § 9¼ ×6¹¹⁄₁₆ in.; 23.2×17 cm. § Inscriptions: *per la Cademia* (in the artist's hand); *Canaletto* (in a nineteenth-century hand). § Provenance: Gamba, 1841; Museo Correr (Lugt, 1862a). § Literature: Pignatti, 1960, p. 35; Constable, 1962, p. 479, no. 626.

The main interest of this fine little drawing by Canaletto is probably, as I have stated, in the inscription, which mentions the Accademia. This clearly means that the two sketches with a staircase were used for the painting (now in the Gallerie dell'Accademia) that Canaletto presented to the Accademia after his election on September 11, 1763. The Venetian courtyard, showing the interior of some trecento building no longer in existence, is drawn in the typical "documentary style," with brilliant effects of light on the sunny façade.

Bernardo Bellotto   1720 – 80

73 COUNTRY LANDSCAPE WITH PEASANTS

Black pencil and pen and sepia. § 10¹⁵⁄₁₆ ×12 in; 27.8×30.5 cm. § Provenance: Frigerio collection; Antonio Morassi collection, Milan (loan 1963; Lugt, 143a).

Bellotto's drawings are generally carefully drawn and rather stiff; rarely do they attain the vibrancy of Canaletto, as does this landscape, which shows a country church surrounded by houses with figures in the foreground. Characteristic wavy lines, in a style similar to the *View of Padua* in the Koenigs collection (Fritzsche, p. 137, fig. 15), confirm an attribution to Bellotto.

Francesco Guardi   1712 – 93

74 MADONNA (6949)

Black chalk heightened with white on brown paper. § 13⅜ ×9⁹⁄₁₆ in.; 34×24.3 cm. § Provenance: Correr, 1830 (Lugt, 461c, 1862a). § Literature: Muraro, 1950, p. 125, fig. 137.

This is one of the few figure drawings that can definitely be attributed to Francesco Guardi, because of its connection with paintings like the signed *Tecchio Madonna* (Moschini, 1956, pl. 19). The characteristic jagged drapery and sharp highlights differ from Gian Antonio Guardi's style, which is noticeably different. The *Tecchio Madonna* is generally thought to be an early work of Francesco, probably dated around the fifties. Some Tiepolesque nuances in the present work might actually strengthen such a hypothesis.

75 THE WEDDING (7294)

Black pencil, pen and sepia, and sepia wash. § 12⁵⁄₁₆ ×10³⁄₁₆ in.; 31.9×25.8 cm. § Provenance: Correr, 1830 (Lugt, 461c, 1862a). § Literature: Byam Shaw, 1933, p. 50; Pallucchini, 1943, p. 37, no. 5; Arslan, 1944, p. 9; Ragghianti, 1953, p. 20.

Francesco made seven sketches related to P. Longhi's series of paintings, *The Sacraments*, which were done between 1750 and 1755 and are now in the Querini Stampalia, Venice. This drawing, together with its six companion pieces, is taken from Pitteri's print, so that the composition is in reverse of the painting. Many attempts have been made to date the drawings; they are generally placed in the early years of Francesco Guardi's career (Pallucchini says around 1756) and are sometimes even attributed to Gian Antonio (i.e., before 1760). However, I would reject the possibility that these drawings are by Antonio, as such tormented modeling and heavy washes are not found in his work. The figures are absolutely Francesco's, and could scarcely be compared to his elder brother's evanescent, flickering forms. As for the date, I would prefer a late one, in the seventies or eighties, for the entire series at the Correr.

76 MADONNA OF THE ROSARY   (4316)
    Pen and sepia and gray wash. § 7⅜ ×6⅞ in.; 18.7×17.4 cm. § Provenance: Cicogna, 1865;
    Museo Correr (Lugt, 1862a). § Literature: Fiocco, 1929, p. 572; Pallucchini, 1943, p. 59, no.
    155; Ragghianti, 1953, p. 20.
No one can doubt that this drawing is a companion piece of the series, *The Sacraments*. Francesco's hand and a very late date are here more apparent, because there is only one step from these little figures to the best-known figure pieces. The resemblance of the saint seen in profile to the bride in the previous drawing is an added proof of this attribution, which differs from the generally accepted one to Gian Antonio Guardi.

77 FOUR PORTRAITS   (685)
    Pen and sepia, and sepia wash on yellowish paper. § 7⁵⁄₁₆ ×10 in.; 18.6×25.4 cm. § Inscription:
    verde; torchin; azuro; laca (in the artist's hand). § Provenance: Correr, 1830 (Lugt, 1862a). §
    Literature: Fiocco, 1923, p. 67; Pallucchini, 1943, p. 40, no. 30; Morassi, 1949, p. 80, figs. 76–79.
A late drawing, dated probably around 1780 on comparison with the painted versions formerly in the Broglio collection in Paris. Judging by the sixteenth-century costumes, these are probably copies from paintings rather than portraits done from life. The head on the left was thought, for some years after Mr. Simonson published the work in 1904 (p. 16), to be Guardi's self-portrait. We now know from Pietro Longhi's portrait of 1764 at the Cà Rezzonico that Guardi was totally different in appearance (Pignatti, 1960, p. 188).

78 THE VISION OF ST. ANTHONY   (731)
    Pen and sepia and sepia wash on gray paper. § 10⁵⁄₁₆ ×6¹⁵⁄₁₆ in.; 26.2×17.6 cm. § Provenance:
    Correr, 1830 (Lugt, 1862a). § Literature: Fiocco, 1923, fig. 14; Pallucchini, 1943, p. 39, no. 19.
One of the most evocative figure drawings by Francesco, in his late style. The painter creates special effects with light washes and shapes the contours with a skipping line, which suggests rather than describes the visual form.

79 ST. MICHAEL   (4620)
    Red chalk. § 9⅞ ×8⅜ in.; 25 ×21.2 cm. § Provenance: Correr, 1830 (Lugt, 461d, 1862a). §
    Literature: Byam Shaw, 1933, p. 48; Pallucchini, 1943, p. 39, no. 24; Gioseffi, 1957, p. 101;
    Pignatti, 1963. § Exhibitions: Fondazione Cini, Venice, 1962, no. 104.
This drawing is one of the most important keys to distinguishing between the work of the two Guardi brothers. Executed as a frontispiece for a book for Duke Renier's election in 1779, eighteen years after Gian Antonio's death, it is indisputably a work of Francesco. Nonetheless, it is still a problematic work. As I wrote in connection with the recent exhibition of this drawing in Venice,

48

there are only a few other sheets with which it can be compared. None of these is in any way connected with Gian Antonio's paintings. The present drawing is not a study for the organ screen in the church of Angelo Raffaele in Venice; the few iconographical resemblances it bears are insufficient for attribution (Pignatti, 1963). In my catalogue of Gian Antonio Guardi's drawings (1957, pp. 29–32), I have given some universally accepted examples of his style when working in chalk. In the case of the *Aurora* and *Minerva* (no. 27, now in the Spector collection, New York), I have related them to paintings in the Cini collection and the Cà Rezzonico. More recently, I have published a preparatory drawing for the organ screen in the church of Angelo Raffaele in Venice from the Accademia Carrara in Bergamo, which looks unmistakably like the *Aurora* and other chalk drawings by Antonio—another proof that the organ screen is his and not Francesco's (Pignatti, 1963).

The differences between the present drawing and Gian Antonio's sheets are significant, although they might escape an inadequately trained eye. Francesco's lines are usually strong and reworked, and the contours are broken and irregular; Gian Antonio's drawings, on the other hand, are always fluent and flickering, soft and loose.

80 THE VISIT   (897)
    Pen and sepia and sepia wash on yellowish paper. § 5 1/16 ×6 7/8 in.; 12.9×17.4 cm. § Provenance: Correr, 1830 (Lugt, 1862a). § Literature: Settecento Italiano, 1932, fig. 183; Pallucchini, 1943, p. 47; Byam Shaw, 1951, p. 67. § Exhibitions: Settecento Italiano, Venice, 1929, no. 8; Fondazione Cini, Venice, 1962, no. 88; National Museum, Stockholm, 1962, no. 310.
The palace where the reception takes place, with a large coat of arms over the portal, is a free sketch of Palazzo Surian at the Cannaregio. Two other versions of this subject are in the Correr (no. 902) and the Cooper Union Museum, New York (Clarke, 1937, no. 35). Byam Shaw states that all of these drawings were used for a painting, now in the Frick Collection, New York. This sheet is a favorite among Guardi drawings, not only for its gondolas and carnival-masked patricians, but also for its own beauty created by light pen touches and iridescent washes.

81 FOUR STRUGGLING FIGURES   (1215)
    Pen and sepia on blue paper. § 3 9/16 ×4 1/4 in.; 9.1×10.9 cm. § Provenance: Correr, 1830 (Lugt, 1862a).
A small unpublished drawing of first-rate quality in its genre. Francesco's line can be distinguished from his imitators (especially from his son Giacomo) by its special resiliency and swiftness.

82 LANDSCAPE WITH PEASANTS AND VILLAGE   (1206)
    Pen and sepia and sepia wash. § 12 1/4 ×9 in.; 31.2×22.8 cm. § Provenance: Correr, 1830 (Lugt, 1862a). § Literature: Lorenzetti, 1936, no. 149; Pallucchini, 1943, p. 54, no. 118; Ragghianti, 1953, no. 19.
As Pallucchini states, the *Landscape* at the Fogg Museum (no. 320) is stylistically identical with this one. Both drawings are by Francesco, despite the fact that the date of the sonnet on the back of this drawing is later than 1798, after Francesco's death. Pallucchini conjectures that the sonnet is by the artist's son Vincenzo Guardi, a priest who wrote poems of mediocre merit about the election of a new parish priest. It is not impossible that the drawing was used for such a purpose, considering the lack of interest in Guardi's drawings in the eighteenth century. Professor Ragghianti disagrees with Pallucchini's theory; he proposes Giacomo as the artist. As a matter of fact, the Correr owns a copy

of the Fogg Museum *Landscape* by Giacomo (no. 62, as orally stated by Miss Mongan) which is very different from the drawing here. The copy demonstrates how poor landscapes by the younger Guardi can be.

83   THE GUARDI HOUSE AT MASTELLINA (689)

Pen and sepia on gray paper. § 8¾ ×6⅞ in.; 21.4×17.5 cm. § Provenance: Correr, 1830 (Lugt, 1862a). § Literature: Lorenzetti, 1936, no. 130; Pallucchini, 1943, p. 56, no. 130; De Maffei, 1948, nos. 23, 42.

This sheet shows the house, which is still standing, of the Guardi family at Mastellina, the birthplace of Francesco's noble ancestors. As De Maffei stated, Francesco Guardi made a trip to his native region as an old man, in 1778. Other drawings are related to that trip, namely sketches along the Valsugana, with *Borgo* (formerly Dubois collection), *Levico* (belonging to Mrs. Stralem), *Borgo and Castle Giovanelli* (owned by Mrs. James Byam Shaw), and *Castel Cogolo* in the Correr (no. 668; Byam Shaw, 1962, p. 77).

84   A STORM AT SEA (1220)

Pen and sepia and sepia wash on gray paper. § 7⅝ ×13 3⁄16 in.; 19.3 ×33.5 cm. § Provenance: Correr, 1830 (Lugt, 1862a). § Literature: Damerini, 1912, pl. xlii; Pallucchini, 1943, p. 58, no. 153.

Francesco Guardi often painted tempest scenes. This particular drawing was probably used for a painting now in the Gasparini collection, Venice (Pallucchini, 1941, pl. xx). The left side appears again in a similar drawing at the Staedelsches Kunstinstitut, Frankfurt.

85   A PORCH WITH FIGURES (716)

Pen and sepia and sepia wash. § 8⅛ ×5¾ in.; 20.7×14.6 cm. § Inscriptions: . . . *di S. Gio. et Paulo* (Director Barozzi's writing, nineteenth century). § Provenance: Correr, 1830 (Lugt, 1862a). § Literature: Settecento Italiano, 1932, fig. 190; Pallucchini, 1943, p. 47, no. 72. § Exhibitions: Settecento Italiano, Venice, 1929, no. 8.

One of the most evocative Guardi drawings, showing a courtyard of the Monastery of San Giovanni e Paolo, according to the as yet undeciphered inscription.

86   A DOORWAY WITH FIGURES (710)

Pen and sepia and wash. § 7⅝ ×5 13⁄16 in.; 19.5×14.8 cm. § Provenance: Correr, 1830 (Lugt, 1862a). § Literature: Settecento Italiano, 1932, fig. 189; Pallucchini, 1943, p. 47, no. 71. § Exhibitions: Settecento Italiano, Venice, 1929, no. 8.

This undulating drawing seems closely related to some of the *capricci* in the Accademia Carrara in Bergamo, probably dating in the eighties (Moschini, 1956, pl. 182). The dramatic juxtaposition of bright and shaded areas is obtained by setting off graded ink washes against blank areas.

87   DESIGN FOR A PARADE GONDOLA (61)

Red chalk on blue-gray paper. § 8 ×15½ in.; 20.1 ×39.1 cm. § Provenance: Correr, 1830 (Lugt, 1862a). § Literature: Lorenzetti, 1936, no. 38; Pallucchini, 1943, p. 52, no. 105. § Exhibitions: National Museum, Stockholm, 1962, no. 313.

Guardi made many designs for elaborate gondolas and *bissone*, special festival boats that were used mostly for the regatta train or receptions for ambassadors. Some of these drawings were used for paintings, but this sketch has not previously been identified. The same boat does however appear in two paintings: the *Bucintoro* in Copenhagen and the *Gondola Train* in Boston. In both pictures the gondola occupies a focal position and therefore probably belonged to an important person, perhaps an ambassador.

88   THE POLIGNAC WEDDING   (30)

Black pencil, pen and sepia, and sepia wash. § 10³⁄₁₆ ×15⁹⁄₁₆ in.; 25.9 ×39.6 cm. § Inscriptions: *Chiesa del nob. H. Gradenigo a Carpenedo, ed il Sposalizio del figlio del Duca di Polignac* (in Director Barozzi's hand, nineteenth century). § Provenance: Correr, 1830 (Lugt, 1862a). § Literature: Fiocco, 1923, no. 81; Pallucchini, 1943, p. 51, no. 97. § Exhibitions: Petit Palais, Paris, 1960, no. 315; Fondazione Cini, Venice, 1962, no. 99.

The Correr has three drawings showing the Polignac wedding, which took place on September 6, 1790. Evidently, Francesco Guardi was asked to prepare some documentary paintings of that event. This version is a general sketch of the church, executed on the spot together with a detail of the priest and the couple (no. 1201). From these, he made the large colored sheet (cat. no. 89), which is probably the *modello*. No reference to the paintings has been found, so it is probable that they were never executed. This is one of the last drawings by Francesco Guardi, made only two years before his death. The vivid ease of his pen strokes is astonishing.

89   THE POLIGNAC WEDDING   (1202)

Black pencil, pen and sepia, and colored washes. § 9 ⅞ ×17 ⅞ in.; 25 ×45.5 cm. § Inscriptions (on the back): *Chiesa del N. H. Gradenigo a Carpenedo; nella fonzione delli sponsali del figlio del Duca Polignac* (in the artist's hand). § Literature: Lorenzetti, 1936, no. 100; Pallucchini, 1943, p. 51, no. 99.

90   THE POLIGNAC WEDDING BANQUET   (29)

Black pencil, pen and sepia, and colored washes. § 10 ⅞ ×16 ½ in.; 27.5 ×41.9 cm. § Inscriptions: *Sala del Nob. H. Gradenigo a Carpenedo coll' apparato dei convitati alle nozze del Polignac* (in Director Barozzi's hand, nineteenth century). § Provenance: Zoppetti; Museo Correr (Lugt, 1862a). § Literature: Damerini, 1912, pl. xxxii; Pallucchini, 1943, p. 51, no. 100. § Exhibitions: Petit Palais, Paris, 1960, no. 314; Fondazione Cini, Venice, 1962, no. 100.

This sheet is a most delightful sketch, a true document of contemporary society. The outlines were probably drawn on the spot, the washes and colors applied later, and the finished sketch finally submitted to the patron for approval. Such documentary projects are typical of Guardi's late years. He did four paintings of the visit of Pope Pius VI in 1782 and six more in the same year to record the official visit of the *Conti del Nord*, Archduke Paul Fedorow of Russia and his wife Mary. No relation can be found between this work and a drawing in the Hermitage of a banquet, which might possibly be by Giacomo Guardi (Lazareff, 1934, pl. v).

91   THE FIRE AT SAN MARCUOLA   (199)

Pen and sepia, and sepia wash on yellowish paper. § 12⅛ ×17⅝ in.; 30.9 ×44.8 cm. § Inscriptions: *Incendio di San Marcuola. L'anno 1789 28 Xbre, Guardi F.* (in the artist's hand?). § Provenance: Correr, 1830, Museo Correr (Lugt, 1862a). § Literature: Damerini, 1912, pl. xl; Pallucchini, 1943, p. 50, no. 96; Byam Shaw, 1951, p. 68. § Exhibitions: Settecento Italiano, Venice, 1929, no. 8; Burlington House, London, 1930, no. 324.

The famous fire that burned a part of the San Marcuola district in 1789 occasioned many documentary drawings and paintings. Our sketch illustrates the beginning of the fire, when it was still limited to the lower part of the houses. It was used for the painting formerly in the Vom Rath collection, Amsterdam. A second unpublished version in colored tempera was in the De Navarro collection, Glen Head, New York. The Metropolitan Museum has a different version of the fire, a pen drawing, which according to Pallucchini shows a later moment, when the flames have spread all around and the firemen are working on the roofs. A corresponding painting exists in the Brambilla collection, Milan (Pallucchini, 1941, pl. XL).

Byam Shaw has recently proposed that the houses in the Correr drawing were added later by Giacomo. This theory was probably suggested by the different densities of the ink, which is somewhat faded in the architecture and darker in the foreground figures. In my opinion, this effect might be the result of the artist's having worked on the drawing at two different times, and I would still attribute the sketch to Francesco alone. In any case, the inscription is definitely not in Giacomo's hand, but very probably in Francesco's (compare with cat. nos. 6 and 94).

92 DOLFIN PALACE AND THE RIALTO   (1197)

    Pen and sepia on gray paper. § 8 7/8 × 6 1/4 in.; 22.5 × 16 cm. § Provenance: Correr, 1830 (Lugt, 461c, 461d, 1862a). § Literature: Pallucchini, 1943, p. 47, no. 78.

Only one of the Palazzo Dolfin's two floors is shown. An atmospheric masterpiece, in Guardi's late style.

93 THE FENICE THEATER   (724)

    Pen and sepia and gray wash. § 7 11/16 × 10 in.; 20 × 25.4 cm. § Inscriptions: *Fenice* (in the artist's hand). § Provenance: Correr, 1830 (Lugt, 1862a). § Literature: Damerini, 1912, pl. LVI; Pallucchini, 1943, p. 49, no. 87. § Exhibitions: Settecento Italiano, Venice, 1929, no. 8; Petit Palais, Paris, 1960, no. 316; Fondazione Cini, Venice, 1962, no. 70.

Francesco twice sketched the Fenice theater, which was inaugurated on May 16, 1792, a few months before his death. This is an extraordinary piece, with its dazzling blank walls and silvery sky with drifting clouds. A second drawing, of similar size, is in the Metropolitan Museum.

Giacomo Guardi   *1764 – 1835*

94 THE DUCAL PALACE AND THE RIVA DEGLI SCHIAVONI   (193)

    Pen and sepia and gray wash on gray paper. § 14 1/2 × 19 7/8 in.; 36 × 50 cm. § Inscriptions: *Veduta del pallazzo Ducale e Zecca e Riva de Schiavoni; Guardi F.* (in the artist's hand). § Provenance: Correr, 1830 (Lugt, 1862a).

An unpublished album sheet, one of many now at the Correr depicting Venetian sights for the foreigners. After a probable collaboration with his father, Giacomo's activity was restricted mainly to this kind of work. Sometimes his style intentionally imitates his father's, and we can mention, among drawings that have been given to Francesco (but are closer to this one), the Querini Stampalia *Piazza San Marco* (Byam Shaw, 1962, no. 69), and the Ingram *Redentore* (*ibid.*, no. 67), whose date I have established as being later than 1819 (Pignatti, 1963).

95 THE BUCINTORO NEAR SANT'ANDREA   (60)

    Pen and sepia on blue-gray paper. § 8 5/8 × 15 3/4 in.; 23 × 40 cm. § Provenance: Zoppetti, 1952; Museo Correr (Lugt, 1862a). § Literature: Damerini, 1912, pl. XXXVII; Pallucchini, 1943, p. 52, no. 101; Ragghianti, 1953, p. 19.

This drawing seems related to paintings such as the Stramezzi *Bucintoro* of the 1780's (Moschini, 1956, pl. 184). A drawing by Francesco Guardi at the Metropolitan Museum shows a similar view of the Bucintoro (Benesch, 1947, no. 67). But can we maintain the traditional attribution to Francesco Guardi? Professor Ragghianti doubted it in his recent essay on Guardi drawings, and we can now add further evidence, having identified the "faking" character of Giacomo Guardi's work. Among Giacomo's distinctive features is the peculiar swarming effect of figures, with curious pin-shaped limbs. No difference exists between our *Bucintoro* and the Ingram *Redentore*, which has been demonstrated as being definitely by Giacomo and painted after 1819 (Pignatti, 1963).

96   THE RIALTO BRIDGE   (5077)
     Pen and black ink and brush and tempera. § 4¼ ×7 in.; 10.9 ×17.8 cm. § Provenance:
     Busetto; Museo Correr (Lugt, 1862a).

An unpublished colored "postcard" by Giacomo. This type of drawing, typical of his late, nineteenth-century period, is sometimes finer than one might think due to the light effects and high quality of glazes.

97   LANDSCAPE WITH PEASANTS   (62)
     Black pencil, pen and sepia, and sepia wash on yellowish paper. § 12⅝ ×9¼ in.; 32 ×23.5 cm.
     § Inscriptions: *Il dipinto è a Padova presso il sig. Lazzari, agosto 1852 (nota retroscritta di V. Lazari)*
     (in a nineteenth-century hand). § Provenance: Zoppetti; Museo Correr (Lugt, 1862a).

This is Giacomo's copy of the identical drawing by Francesco, now at the Fogg Museum (no. 320). As mentioned in cat. no. 82, the comparison between these two drawings gives a clue for distinguishing the personalities of the two Guardis.

Gian Battista Tiepolo   1696 – 1770

98   STUDY OF A STANDING GENTLEMAN   (7074)
     Red chalk heightened with white on blue-gray paper. § 17¾ ×11¼ in.; 44.5 ×28.5 cm. §
     Provenance: Gatteri, 1885; Museo Correr (Lugt, 461c, 461d, 1862a). § Literature: Lorenzetti,
     1946, p. 10, no. 16 *verso*.

G. B. Tiepolo worked in the Würzburg Residence from October 1750 to November 1753, with the assistance of his sons Domenico and Lorenzo and the Italian stucco decorator, Antonio Bossi. A sketchbook of eighty-seven pages, which are among the large number of chalk drawings connected with the frescoes at Würzburg, came to the Correr from the painter Lorenzo Gatteri. After it had been broken up, Lorenzetti re-established its original order and published a facsimile edition in 1946. On the last page, an authentic inscription gives the names of G. B. and Domenico Tiepolo and the price of the sketchbook in 1770—eight sequins, which Byam Shaw calculates to be worth around twelve dollars (1962, p. 22). This inscription is evidence that the sketchbook does contain drawings by both Gian Battista and Domenico; scholars have long endeavored to distinguish between them. In his recent book on Domenico's drawings, Byam Shaw masterfully summarizes the results of this research, which was discussed in the introduction to this catalogue. The examples from the Correr sketchbook that follow have been selected to illustrate draftsmanship of the two Tiepolos.

   This drawing is a study for the portrait of Antonio Bossi included in the Würzburg staircase fresco by Gian Battista. The substantial differences in the legs and drapery, as well as in the detail of the sitter's portrait, are proof that the drawing was made *for* and not *after* the fresco and, consequently, is by Gian Battista.

99 STUDY OF TWO GLOVED HANDS   (7098)

Red chalk heightened with white on blue-gray paper. § 17⅞ ×11¼ in.; 44.9×28.5 cm. § Provenance: Gatteri, 1885; Museo Correr (Lugt, 461c, 461d, 1862a). § Literature: Lorenzetti, 1946, p. 13, no. 40 *verso*; Vigni, 1956, p. 365; Byam Shaw, 1962, p. 24.

One of the most difficult problems in the sketchbook puzzle. This drawing is closely related to the hands of the bishop in the *Barbarossa Wedding* in Würzburg. Some slight variations could be interpreted as proof that the drawing was made *for* and not copied *after* the fresco, which has always been attributed to Gian Battista.

The difficulty comes from the existence of another similar pair of hands in the sketchbook (no. 7071; Lorenzetti no. 13 *verso*), which has been related to a Würzburg lunette with St. Ambrose, probably a work by Domenico (Vigni, 1956, p. 365). A final explanation is not easily found, as we might even have two drawings by Gian Battista, subsequently used for paintings by both artists. The creative, fluid lines in this drawing are an indication that it was done by Gian Battista.

100 STUDY OF A MALE FIGURE   (7140)

Red chalk heightened with white on blue-gray paper. § 17½ ×11¼ in.; 44.5×28.5 cm. § Provenance: Gatteri, 1885; Museo Correr (Lugt, 1862, 461c, 461d, 1862a). § Literature: Lorenzetti, 1946, p. 17, no. 82 *verso*. § Exhibitions: Mostra di Tiepolo, Venice, 1951, no. 60; Petit Palais, Paris, 1960, no. 42.

One of the most striking figures for the Würzburg decoration, probably an Oriental in the Africa fresco on the great staircase. A faint suggestion of a turban can be seen over the figure's head.

101 STUDY OF A MALE NUDE AND A FEMALE HEAD   (7144)

Red chalk heightened with white on blue-gray paper. § 17½ ×11¼ in.; 44.5×28.5 cm. § Provenance: Gatteri, 1885; Museo Correr (Lugt, 461c, 461d, 1862a). § Literature: Lorenzetti 1946, p. 17, no. 86; Byam Shaw, 1962, p. 22. § Exhibitions: Mostra di Tiepolo, Venice, 1951, no. 62.

One of the finest heads in the Gatteri sketchbook, which Byam Shaw also attributes to Gian Battista because of the sense of forms expressed with extreme economy of line. However, many of these composite sketches are by the son (compare with cat. no. 107).

102 STUDY OF A GENERAL   (7393)

Red chalk on blue paper. § 9½ ×16⅛ in.; 15.5×24 cm. § Provenance: Correr, 1830 (Lugt, 461c, 1862a).

An unpublished drawing from a newly discovered group at the Correr Museum, this was probably part of a sketchbook on thin blue paper that has now been broken up. Its interest is greater than its beauty, but we thought it useful to show this drawing because it is the third one related to the central figure in the great staircase fresco at Würzburg. It is considered a portrait of architect Balthasar Neumann (Von Freeden-Lamb, 1956, figs. 42–43). The figure is exactly the same as the fresco, and probably the sketch was a record drawn from the scaffolding; this would explain the presence of the sitter's feet, which cannot be seen from below (an astute suggestion by J. Byam Shaw, 1962, p. 26). The first drawing, in Berlin, shows the general reclining in a different pose from that in the fresco;

54

the quality is superb and the lines are free and flowing. The second drawing, now in the Würzburg Museum, is one of the characteristic composite sheets by Domenico. Our drawing is certainly by the same hand as the Berlin drawing by Gian Battista.

103   STUDY OF LEGS   (7404)
   Red chalk heightened with white on blue paper. § 12⅝ ×6⁵⁄₁₆ in.; 32×16 cm. § Provenance: Correr, 1830 (Lugt, 461c, 1862a).

The fine quality and characteristics corresponding to the preceding drawing suggest an attribution to Gian Battista during his Würzburg period (1750–53).

104   FOUR FEMALE NUDES   (203)
   Black pencil, pen and sepia, and sepia wash heightened with white. § 8⅝ ×7¼ in; 22×18.5 cm. § Inscriptions: *Tiepolo: 10* (in the artist's hand); *G. B. Tiepolo* (in an eighteenth-century hand). § Provenance: Correr, 1830 (Lugt, 1862a).

A fine, unpublished pen drawing, probably a study for fountain or balustrade sculptures, on the order, for instance, of the Thyssen *Death of Hyacinth* (c. 1753). In style and in its second inscription, perhaps written by Orloff, this drawing is closely related to the Birtschansky *Nymphs* (Cailleux, 1952, p. 41, pl. 3).

105   CARICATURE OF A GENTLEMAN   (7037)
   Pen and sepia and sepia wash. § 7⁹⁄₁₆ ×3¾ in.; 19.2×9.5 cm. § Provenance: Correr, 1830 (Lugt, 1862a).

Although it is always difficult to distinguish the caricatures of Gian Battista from those of Domenico, it can be done if one keeps in mind the main differences between their styles. The fluid, vibrant lines and the strong light effects in this drawing are characteristic of the father.

Domenico Tiepolo   1727 – 1805

106   STUDY OF A HUNCHBACK   (7133)
   Red chalk heightened with white on blue-gray paper. § 17½ ×11½ in.; 44.5×28.5 cm. § Provenance: Gatteri, 1885; Museo Correr (Lugt, 461c, 461d, 1862a). § Literature: Lorenzetti, 1946, p. 16, no. 75; Pignatti, 1951, p. 196; Byam Shaw, 1962, p. 73. § Exhibitions: Mostra di Tiepolo, Venice, 1951, p. 110.

Once again we go to the Gatteri sketchbook; this time to look at examples of Domenico's work. This study can be attributed to him with certainty since it is the reverse of one of the people in Domenico's seventh etching of the *Flight into Egypt* series (as noted by Byam Shaw). Domenico's style is noticeable in the heavy, reworked lines and a certain hesitancy of the contours.

107   STUDIES FOR A BOY READING   (7104)
   Red chalk heightened with white on blue-gray paper. § 17½ ×11¼ in.; 44.5×28.5 cm. § Provenance: Gatteri, 1885; Museo Correr (Lugt, 461c, 461d, 1862a). § Literature: Lorenzetti, 1946, p. 13, no. 46.

A typical composite sheet, which shows Domenico's weak line and insistent shading.

108   STUDIES FOR A SLEEPING BOY AND A CARICATURE   (7129)
   Red chalk heightened with white on blue-gray paper. § 11¼ ×17½ in.; 44.5×28.5 cm. § Inscriptions: *Loren* (in the artist's hand). § Provenance: Gatteri, 1885, Museo Correr (Lugt, 461c, 461d, 1862a). § Literature: Lorenzetti, 1946, p. 16, no. 71; Byam Shaw, 1962, p. 22.

Comparing this sketch to preceding cat. nos. 106 and 107, we ascribe it to Domenico rather than Gian Battista (as does Byam Shaw, 1962, p. 22). Its *verso* shows a coughing old man, who appears in Domenico's *Last Supper* in Desenzano. It is amusing to note the pig's face, presumably a sketch of Domenico's young brother Lorenzo, whose name is scribbled between the long ears.

109 STUDY OF HANDS   (7063)
Red chalk heightened with white on blue-gray paper. § 17½× ×11⅜ in.; 44.5 ×28.5 cm. §
Provenance: Gatteri, 1885; Museo Correr (Lugt, 461c, 461d, 1862a). § Literature: Lorenzetti,
1946, p. 9, no. 5.

The difference between this and cat. no. 99 by Gian Battista must be evident. Domenico's loose touch hesitates on the surfaces and along the contours, with mediocre results.

110 GOD THE FATHER   (6005)
Pen and gray ink and sepia wash. § 9¹⁄₁₆ ×6¾ in.; 23.1 ×17.3 cm. § Inscriptions: *Dom. Tiepolo F.* (in the artist's hand); 71 (in an eighteenth-century hand). § Provenance: Gatteri; Museo Correr (Lugt, 461c, 1862a). § Literature: Byam Shaw, 1962, p. 32.

Domenico Tiepolo drew many variations of God the Father in clouds supported by angels and cherubs; Byam Shaw lists nearly twenty, fourteen of which are at the Correr, but adds that nearly sixty are known to him. Evidently, since they are numbered in the upper left corner, the original series totaled 102. This particular one exemplifies Domenico's best album-drawing style of the nineties, with its masterful use of the pen and graded washes.

111 CARICATURE   (7038)
Pen and sepia and gray wash. § 6⅞ ×5⅛ in.; 17.6 ×13.0 cm. § Provenance: Correr, 1830 (Lugt, 1862a). § Literature: Valcanover, 1960, no. 447. § Exhibitions: Petit Palais, Paris, 1960, no. 447.

A typical caricature by Domenico, distinguished from his father's work by the uniform character of the line and the whitish light. Nos. 234, 235, and 236 in the Trieste Museum seem very similar to this work, which dates from the late decades of the eighteenth century (Vigni, 1942, pp. 72–73).

112 THE BALLAD SINGERS   (6042)
Black pencil, pen and sepia, and sepia wash. § 14¾ ×19⅞ in.; 37.5 ×50.5 cm. § Inscriptions: *Dom. Tiepolo f. 1791* (in the artist's hand). § Provenance: Cantalamessa; Museo Correr (Lugt, 1862a). § Literature: Pignatti, 1951, p. 196. § Exhibitions: Mostra di Tiepolo, Venice, 1951, no. 128.

This is one of the best of Domenico's drawings of contemporary scenes, most of which he executed in the seventeen-nineties. Byam Shaw states that no less than twenty of these works bear like this one the date 1791 (1962, p. 47). Domenico no doubt intended these drawings to be grotesque and satirical. He probably patterned them after his father's caricatures, making free copies in an imitative manner but more ambitious in scale. These sheets are generally of a large size (approximately 15 ×20 in.) enclosed by a margin; they possess the quality of finished pictorial compositions. Some of the most significant drawings are in the Talleyrand collection, in the museums of Boston, Minneapolis, Cleveland, and Hartford, and in private collections, particularly in France (Byam Shaw, 1962, nos. 59–77). Domenico's *Punchinello* series—over one hundred drawings, now widely dispersed—was probably also done in the nineties. The actual subject of the *Ballad Singers* remains unknown but is

56

most likely more than a grotesque double serenade for two voices and quartet. Some popular elements in the lady's dress indicate a street show.

Lorenzo Tiepolo *1736 – 76*

113 HEAD OF AN OLD MAN (1337)
Red chalk heightened with white on gray paper. § 9¾ ×6⅞ in.; 24.8 ×17.6 cm. § Provenance: Zoppetti, 1852; Museo Correr (Lugt, 461d, 1862a).

An unpublished work, this head is a copy of a drawing by Gian Battista now in the Weimar Museum (Hadeln, 1927, pl. 169). The careful attention to detail, the looseness of the total effect, and, further, the fine quality of this study lead us to attribute it to Lorenzo Tiepolo. He often copied his father, mainly when making etchings (Byam Shaw, 1962, no. 27). Works known to be by Lorenzo are in the museums of Würzburg and Pavia and the Scholz and Rasini collections (Pignatti, 1951, p. 198).

Pier Antonio Novelli *1729 – 1804*

114 APOLLO WITH POETS (3661)
Red pencil, pen and black ink, and gray wash. § 9½ ×6⅝ in.; 24 ×16.9 cm. § Provenance: Correr, 1830 (Lugt, 1862a).

A fine unpublished drawing by Novelli, which shows his best finished style, probably made for a title page or book illustration. The subject—five poets and a poetess paying homage to Apollo—is unique. The origins of Novelli's drawing style—and of his paintings as well—can be traced to the Pellegrini-Diziani school. There is also some influence of Fontebasso in his shading, but the main characteristic of his style is probably his interest in Rembrandt. Novelli's son Francesco later reproduced heads by Rembrandt in a famous edition of prints. Large collections of Novelli's drawings are now in the Correr, Albertina, Cooper Union, Princeton University, and Detroit museums and in the Scholz collection.

115 HEAD OF A YOUNG MAN (1556)
Black pencil on gray paper. § 10 ×6⅛ in.; 25.5 ×15.6 cm. § Provenance: Correr, 1830 (Lugt, 1862a).

Resembling classical sculpture, this head shows a marked liveliness, created by the sparkling touch of line. We can compare it to pen drawings such as the *Head of a Man* in Bassano (Riva 515; Magagnato, 1956, p. 72).

116 POPULAR SCENES (1436)
Pen and black ink and black wash. § 8⅝ ×12⅜ in.; 21.9 ×31.5 cm. § Provenance: Zoppetti, 1852, Museo Correr (Lugt 461c, 1862a).

This unpublished sheet is part of a series, two of which are now in Warsaw. They were probably intended as book illustrations. Also tentatively attributed to Piazzetta (Mrozinska, 1958, pp. 52–53).

Francesco Novelli *1767 – 1836*

117 WEDDING BANQUET (1599)
Black pencil, pen and sepia, and brush and colored washes on yellowish paper. § 8¼ ×9⅞ in.; 21 ×25 cm. § Inscriptions: *Frº Novelli* (in the artist's hand). § Provenance: Correr, 1830 (Lugt, 1862a).

57

Francesco Novelli, Pier Antonio's son, worked primarily as an etcher in Venice and Rome. He was a pupil of the renowned French etcher De Non, who was active in Venice in the last decade of the eighteenth century. Francesco's works show a special finesse and taste for illustration. This unpublished drawing is a fine example of his style when working in pencil, pen, and colored washes.

Francesco Bartolozzi   1728 – 1815

118   CHERUB WITH COMPASS   (1379)

Red chalk on yellowish paper. § 8 ×8 in.; 20.3 ×20.3 cm. § Inscriptions: *Franc.º Bartolozzi 20* (in the artist's hand). § Provenance: Zoppetti, 1852; Museo Correr (Lugt, 461c, 1862a).

An unpublished drawing by the prolific engraver Francesco Bartolozzi, who received his training in Venice at Joseph Wagner's shop from 1745 to 1760. The Albertina owns a large group of his drawings: nos. 445 and 447 are stylistically similar to this work. Born in Florence, Bartolozzi was an eclectic in Venice, mixing skillfully the styles of Pittoni, Tiepolo, and Novelli.

Antonio Zucchi   1726 – 95

119   PORTRAIT OF A CARDINAL   (822)

Black and red pencil. § 5 ⅝ ×4 ⅞ in.; 14.3 ×12.3 cm. § Inscriptions: *Zucchi* (probably in the artist's hand). § Provenance: Correr, 1830 (Lugt, 1862a).

The old inscription, which may be a signature, points to the famous family of painters and engravers active since the late seventeenth century—beginning with Andrea Zucchi, followed by his brother Francesco, father of Antonio. The obvious relationship of this fine portrait, which appears to be a preparatory study for a title page, with both Neoclassic taste and Venetian style, points to the name of Antonio Zucchi. Zucchi studied in Venice under Amigoni, then visited London, where he married Angelica Kauffmann. The various influences to which he was exposed all figure in his refined draftsmanship.

Bernardino Bison   1762 – 1844

120   SKETCH OF SEVEN HEADS   (1355)

Brush and sepia wash and greenish wash. § 5¼ ×7¼ in.; 13.4 ×18.7 cm. § Inscriptions: *Bisson fece scherzando* (in the artist's hand); *17* (nineteenth century). § Provenance: Zoppetti, 1852; Museo Correr (Lugt, 1862a).

Bernardino Bison is perhaps the most interesting Venetian draftsman at the end of the eighteenth century. Many of his drawings—including the superb series in the Cooper Union Museum—are still practically unknown, even after the exhibition devoted to his work in Udine, 1963. Many more are incorrectly attributed because of Bison's tendency to adopt other artist's styles. Other large groups of his drawings are in the Castello Sforzesco, Osio, Milan, and the Miotti collection, Udine. This particular sketch, an unusual example of brush and wash technique, is related to works dating from 1815 through the twenties, such as the *Oriental Girl* in the Miotti collection (Rizzi, 1962, p. 57, no. 63). While Bison's style clearly shows its origins in the Venetian traditions of Pellegrini and Tiepolo, it also reflects early nineteenth-century European movements. Stylistically, this drawing represents the conclusion of eighteenth-century drawing in Venice.

58

Illustrations

I. SEBASTIANO RICCI: The Continence of Scipio

2. SEBASTIANO RICCI: Figure of a Woman

3.   PELLEGRINI: The Judgment of Paris

4. PELLEGRINI: Venus Triumphant

5. GIAN ANTONIO GUARDI: Madonna and Child with Three Saints

6. GIAN ANTONIO GUARDI: February

7. GRASSI: Christ at Calvary

10. PITTONI: The Adoration of the Shepherds

12. PITTONI: The Infant Jesus

13.   AMIGONI: Portrait of a Gentleman

15.   CROSATO: Zephirus and Flora

17. DIZIANI: The Assumption

16. DIZIANI: The Flight into Egypt

18.   DIZIANI: St. Cecilia and a Bishop

19. DIZIANI: The Annunciation

23. BORTOLONI: Susannah

20. DIZIANI: The Holy Trinity and Dominican Saints

22. DIZIANI: Two Bissona Costumes

21. DIZIANI: The Flight into Egypt

26. MARCUOLA: The Victory of Cyrus

27. FONTEBASSO: The Presentation of the Virgin

7.

28.   FONTEBASSO: St. Joseph with the Christ Child

29. FONTEBASSO: Christ and the Woman Taken in Adultery

31. MARIESCHI: The Transfer of the Relics of S. Giovanni Elemosinario

30. TARSIA: The Rape of Proserpina

35. GUARANA: Minerva

33.　GUARANA: Venice Triumphant

36.　PIAZZETTA: Portrait of a Young Man

39. PIAZZETTA: The Dead Christ and Four Saints

40. PIAZZETTA: Lady and Nobleman in Conversation

43. MAGGIOTTO: A Peasant Girl in Profile

41. DALL'OGLIO: St. Joseph and the Christ Child

45. CAPPELLA: A Peasant Girl

47. PIETRO LONGHI: A Peasant Girl Broaching a Cask

49. PIETRO LONGHI: A Lady Spinning

50. PIETRO LONGHI: A Lady Fanning a Gentleman

51. PIETRO LONGHI: A Lady Feeding her Canary

52. PIETRO LONGHI: A Gentleman Bowing

53. PIETRO LONGHI: A Gentleman Seating a Lady

54. PIETRO LONGHI: Hunting in the Lagoon

55.   PIETRO LONGHI: Nurse and Child with a Mirror Frame

59. MARCO RICCI: Landscape with a Mill

57. ALESSANDRO LONGHI: Portrait of Doge Morosini

61. MARCO RICCI: Stage Design with Figures

62. MARCO RICCI: A Soldier

64. SIMONINI: Cavalry Battle

65.   ZAIS: Cavalry Battle

68. ZUCCARELLI: Landscape with Peasants

67. ZAIS: The Rape of Europa

69. ZUCCARELLI: Landscape with Shepherdess

70. CARLEVARIS: Palazzo Labia and Two Sketches of a Gentleman

71. CARLEVARIS: Lagoon with Two Boats

72. CANALETTO: Four Architectural Sketches

73. BELLOTTO: Country Landscape with Peasants

74. FRANCESCO GUARDI: Madonna

78. FRANCESCO GUARDI: The Vision of St. Anthony

76. FRANCESCO GUARDI: Madonna of the Rosary

75. FRANCESCO GUARDI: The Wedding

77. FRANCESCO GUARDI: Four Portraits

79. FRANCESCO GUARDI: St. Michael

80. FRANCESCO GUARDI: The Visit

81.   FRANCESCO GUARDI: Four Struggling Figures

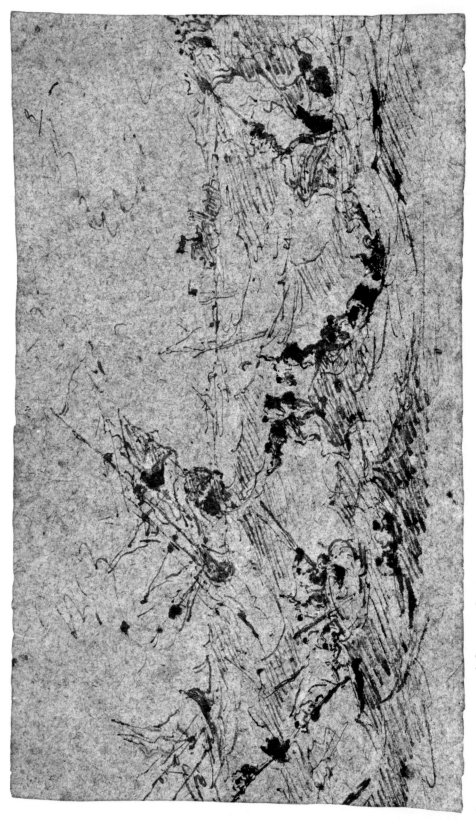

84. FRANCESCO GUARDI: A Storm at Sea

130

83. FRANCESCO GUARDI: The Guardi House at Mastellina

82. FRANCESCO GUARDI: Landscape with Peasants and Village

86.   FRANCESCO GUARDI: A Doorway with Figures

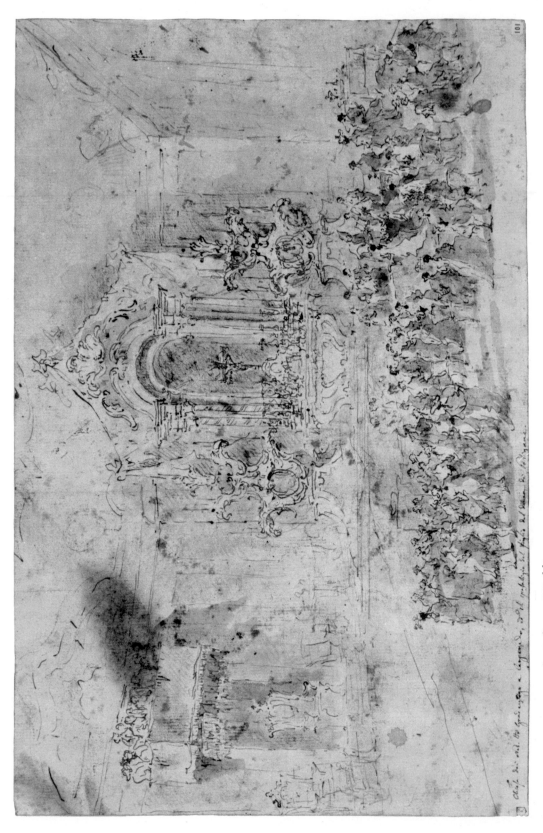

88. FRANCESCO GUARDI: The Polignac Wedding

89.   FRANCESCO GUARDI: The Polignac Wedding

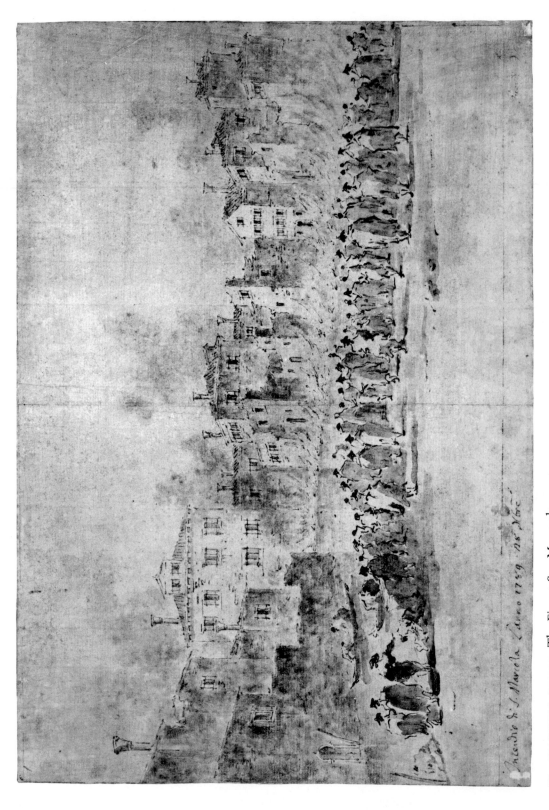

91. FRANCESCO GUARDI: The Fire at San Marcuola

87.　FRANCESCO GUARDI: Design for a Parade Gondola

90.　FRANCESCO GUARDI: The Polignac Wedding Banquet

97. GIACOMO GUARDI: Landscape with Peasants

92. FRANCESCO GUARDI: Dolfin Palace and the Rialto

93. FRANCESCO GUARDI: The Fenice Theatre

96. GIACOMO GUARDI: The Rialto Bridge

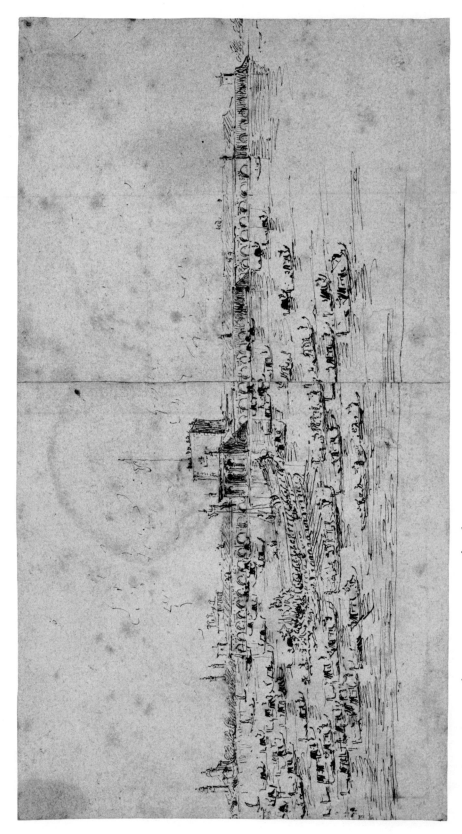

95.   GIACOMO GUARDI: The Bucintoro near Sant'Andrea

98. GIAN BATTISTA TIEPOLO: Study of a Standing Gentleman

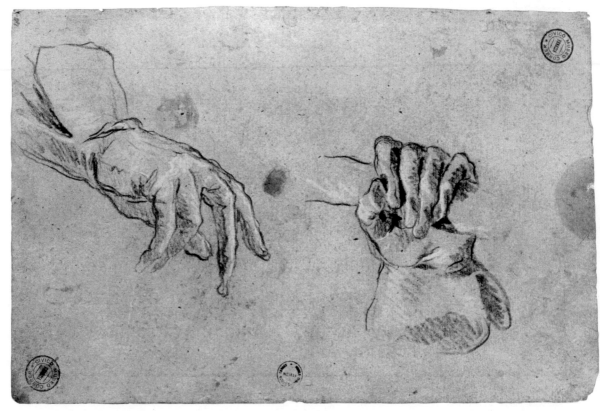

99.   GIAN BATTISTA TIEPOLO: Study of Two Gloved Hands

100.   GIAN BATTISTA TIEPOLO: Study of a Male Figure

102. GIAN BATTISTA TIEPOLO: Study of a General

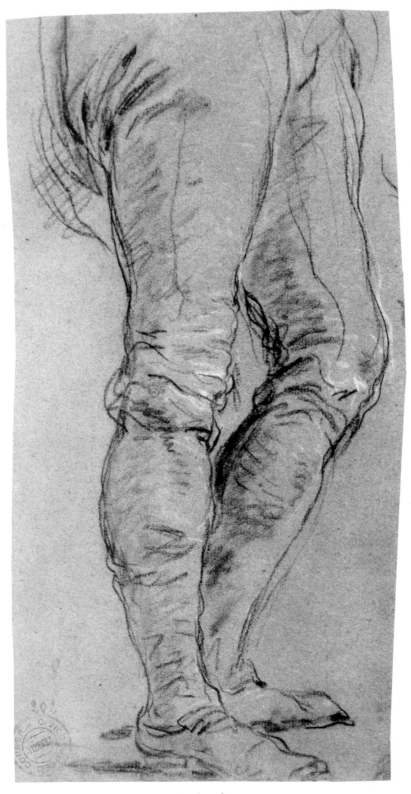

103. GIAN BATTISTA TIEPOLO: Study of Legs

101.   GIAN BATTISTA TIEPOLO: Study of a Male Nude and a Female Head

104. GIAN BATTISTA TIEPOLO: Four Female Nudes

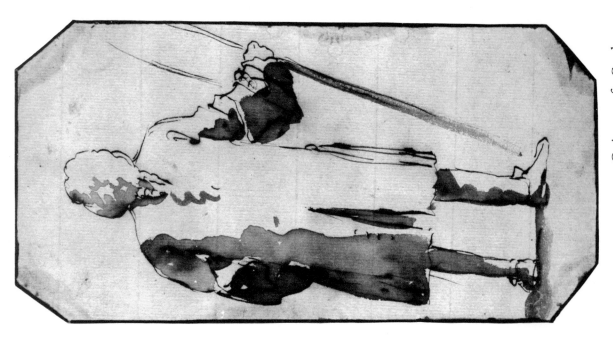

105. GIAN BATTISTA TIEPOLO: Caricature of a Gentleman

111. DOMENICO TIEPOLO: Caricature

106. DOMENICO TIEPOLO: Study of a Hunchback

109. DOMENICO TIEPOLO: Study of Hands

110.   DOMENICO TIEPOLO: God the Father

II2. DOMENICO TIEPOLO: The Ballad Singers

113. LORENZO TIEPOLO: Head of an Old Man

116. PIER ANTONIO NOVELLI: Popular Scenes

114.   PIER ANTONIO NOVELLI: Apollo with Poets

119. ZUCCHI: Portrait of a Cardinal

117. FRANCESCO NOVELLI: Wedding Banquet

120. BISON: Sketch of Seven Heads

Franc.º Bartolozzi 20.

118. BARTOLOZZI: Cherub with Compass

Index of Artists